God ...

JOB

God ... Is GOD

series

God ... Is GOD

JOB

Don't Blame the Victim

Jim Gersetich
Edited by Bethany Gersetich

God Is God Publishing
Brooklyn Center, Minnesota

God Is God Publishing

Brooklyn Center, Minnesota
Copyright © 2019 by Jim Gersetich
All Rights Reserved

Revision 1.2
Copyeditor: Bethany Gersetich
Cover Design: Rebecca Hunt

© 2019 All rights reserved. God ... Is God Publishing. No part of this book may be reproduced in any form by any means without the express permission of the author or publisher.

If you would like to do any of the above (beyond Fair Use provisions in copyright law), please contact the publisher at jim@god-isgod.com.

Published in the United States by God ... is God Publishing.
www.god-isgod.com
ISBN: 978-1-6861-4533-9

Unless otherwise specified, all Scripture quotations are from the New American Standard Bible, Updated Edition 1995.

For my wife, the only woman on the planet for me, for her long-suffering commitment while I whittled away the hours – make those years – writing *God ... Is GOD: JOB*.

Never assume that a calamity is a punishment.

Preface	ix
The story from 40,000 feet	1
1: The Grinch … in the BIBLE?	15
2: Some fun with numbers	21
3: Misery Does NOT Love Company	24
4: the "Spanish Inquisition"	28
5: Bad Things, Good People?	35
6: We're Talking About God!	43
7: Be Comforted	49
8: With friends like this, …	53
9: God is Sovereign; Our Job is to Trust Him	57
10: Incendiary Bombs	60
11: Job's Not-So-Gracious Reply to Zophar	62
12: Eliphaz: "Throwing Bullets"	75
13: Job's Sad Response to Eliphaz	84
14: Bildad Comes Out Guns Blazing	91
15: Job's Brokenness as Response to Bildad	94
16: Zophar's Nuclear Response	100
17: Job Asks Zophar Just To Listen	105
18: Amazing Grace	110
19: Debate's End	112
20: Elihu Enters the Fray	118
21: Elihu: my turn again	123
22: About God …	127
23: Now, I'll Speak – God	132

24: Job rePlies: Whatever 136
25: About God's Mercy 142
26: An Ancient plan 147
27: Reunited 151
Appendix 156
Bibliography 173

INTRODUCTION

I call this book a "read-along." I think the best way to read it is to have your Bible open to the book of Job, and *read* this book *along* with the book of Job.

It's not a study guide or commentary. I wanted to convey the message of Job to normal people, who might not have seen its beauty and message before.

I hope it is not as boring as your regular Job.

PREFACE

The book of Job is amazing. It is a story written between 3500 to 4000 years ago. It's been in play as a story ever since then. And yet as old and well-traveled as it seems, it defies scholars' best attempts to understand it fully today. The author of Job was a literary genius whose writing compares favorably with even the best poets of our modern world.

However, many people are unfamiliar with reading the book for a bunch of little reasons and four huge reasons:

IT'S A STORY ABOUT SUFFERING

Folks sometimes skip Job because of the nature of the story. Some people don't want to read about suffering. This is especially true when the sufferer exhibits a fantastic amount of patience and virtue, even in the middle of his suffering. Such a treatise might hit just a little too close to home, in more ways than one.

Our trials can be bad. But compared to the extreme trials Job endured, our trials can come up a little short. We can lose our employment (as I write this sentence, I've been unemployed for a month), endure severe illnesses, and even lose a loved one. These seem huge. But Job had *all* of those trials and more.

In the face of Job's huge trials, sometimes we simply want to avoid the subject.

IT'S A STORY ABOUT GODLINESS DURING SUFFERING

It gets worse, though, when one considers sermons one might hear dealing with the book. Sermons, by their nature, emphasize obvious points. They deal with less obvious ones, but they always deal with big ones. And one of the most important things about the man Job is that he weathered the storms of his trials *incredibly* well. So, any sermon on Job that is worth its salt is going to tell us about his patience, longsuffering, operating under fire, etc. Job's example is, frankly, unachievable, at least for this author. And, I suspect, for many readers.

This emphasis on Job's quality of character is the second big reason people avoid the book. He's just too *good*[1]; he's beyond anything we can ever hope to achieve. The concentration of the story on his character is painful for us to read, for we know instinctively that we fall short.

As I hope the reader will see, this is very far from being a major point in the book. It is a perception shared by many of us, possibly because that's the biggest thing we've noticed in the book. But to the real meat in Job, this issue is a mere sidelight. The real meat is paradoxically both more difficult to accept and less painful to think about. We'll have more on those later.

BOOOOORING!

The third reason is that some people find the book boring. If one skims it casually or even skims it, it seems repetitive. The chapters in the middle all seem to run together. They all seem to be repeating themselves over and over again. As I hope to show later in this book, the chapters are not so repetitive, after all. They cover some of the same subjects, but they change tone dramatically, becoming harsher and harsher as the book continues.

Further, there is a structure. It's obvious once one notices it or has it pointed out. But if I'm just breezing through the book to get a dozen checkmarks on my *Read the Bible in a year* plan, I'll miss it. That's what occurred in my life. Twice.

---

[1] We think of this kind of "good" as an almost-perfect ideal, but we know all too well that we'll never measure up to it.

IS IT A TRUE STORY?

Fourth, some folks find it hard to believe that the book even tells a true story. In the ivory towers where scholars pore over their scholarly works, there are many disagreements about this book. Disagreements include the book's nature, date of writing, who the authorwas, and a host of others. Scholars even debate verses that might be embellishments.

Most of these scholarly issues can be important and are valuable. But it seems that the Church needs a layman's level treatment that can help people get a handle on the story and the many points it attempts to bring up, but without delving into the scholar-level items any more than is necessary. I hope that *God ... Is GOD: JOB* will help some people achieve an understanding of Job's book that helps them learn more of whatever it is that God would like to teach them through it. And one thing is certain to me: God *does* want to teach people through the Biblical book of Job.

THE STORY FROM 40,000 FEET

Have you ever flown in an airplane? The view from up high can be spectacular. But what I find fascinating is that everything below is so small. Individual people, houses, and even low hills blend together. But we do get a better perspective from there as regards roads and massive terrain changes.

Even cities are hard to visualize, except at night. At night, all the lights are on, and the view is magnificent.

We need a similar vantage point to understand the messages of Job's book fully. The message can be unclear because many of the things the four debate opponents say *seem* right, but, in many cases, could not be further from the truth. Most importantly, it's impossible to get at the heart of the book's message until after reading the last chapter.

THE PROLOGUE

The book of Job starts by describing the man Job a bit, including telling about his wealth and how he maintains his and his family's upright standing before God. First, we see with a view of the throne room of God in Heaven. Then we hear of some of God's servants, presenting themselves to the

Lord. One of these was Satan. God challenges Satan to consider God's servant Job. God opens the conversation about the man Job by saying that Job is righteous and upright on the earth, a man unlike any other.

Satan retorts that Job is only righteous because God has bribed Job. Satan says that if God were to take away Job's stuff, Job would surely curse God to His face. Possibly to the surprise of the readers, God says (paraphrased), *"do your worst."* But He qualifies the trial by saying Satan must not harm Job himself[2].

Back on Earth, with machine-gun efficiency, Job finds out he's lost all 10 of his kids, all of his property (except his house), all of his servants (except four, who delivered the bad news from four different fronts.) In minutes, Job went from a family of twelve and being one of the richest men in the world, to a family of two, stripped of his wealth.

What was Job's response? Did Satan win his cosmic bet with God? Job's stunning response is to praise God. His kids are dead, and his property obliterated, and yet Job blesses God. No wonder God spoke so highly of him!

Next, we return to the throne room of God for round two. God points out to Satan that Job did

---

[2] Note that Satan doesn't mess with Job's wife, either. He knows very well that "the two" have become "one flesh". Therefore, Job's wife is part of Job now, and Satan isn't going to take any chances on hurting her. He wants to win this argument with God; he'll take no risks that might disqualify him.

not curse God. Round one goes to the Lord: Job remained righteous in God's eyes.

Satan says that God rigged the game: God would not let Satan harm the man, but he could only take his stuff away. (It's kind of crass to consider Job's ten kids as just part of Job's possessions, but hey – this is Satan we're talking about.)

Satan again challenges God that if only God allows Satan to harm the man himself, then Job will curse God. To me, it sounds like a kid who just lost a coin toss, following it up by saying, "best two out of three?" The first time I read this, I thought that God would toss the devil out on his ear. But to my shock, God allowed this test as well.

Now, when God gives Satan permission to harm someone, he (unfortunately for his target) does his job very well. He was not allowed to kill Job, but only to harm him. But as Genie says in Disney's *Aladdin*, "you'd be surprised what you can live through." Job is about to suffer a LOT.

So Satan gives Job a painful disease. We cannot identify the disease, but we know that Job had boils all over his skin from head to toe.

They were very painful, and they itched. Naturally, Job scratched them. And when he rubbed them, it broke the skin, and disgusting fluids leaked over his body. Even Job's wife, when she talks to Job, effectively says, "Why don't you just curse God and die." This disease was genuinely awful.

At this point, we enter the heart of the book. But we should note that we do not get to see the throne room of God again. What ultimately happened in heaven? We do not know. We could take some guesses, but it doesn't matter to understand the book. We do see God again at the end of the book. And His statements then shed light on what must have happened in Heaven. But I'm getting ahead of myself.

Before Job's first lamenting speech, we see Job sitting on the road, throwing dust on himself. Tossing dirt on yourself was a method the ancients used to express grief, mostly when grief was severe. The disease resulted in fluids all over Job's body, so the dirt stuck to Job's skin. Eww!

Into this setting, his three friends appear, ostensibly to comfort Job. But from a distance, they cannot even recognize their friend; that is how disgusting this disease was. When they get to him, they sit on the road with him. For seven whole days, the three friends sat with Job in the road dirt, and none of them spoke a word. Job's obvious pain and anguish were just too much for words.

THE DEBATE

After a week of silence, Job finally begins speaking with a lament. He laments his very life, wishing he had never been born, and openly wondering what it was that he had done to deserve such punishment. In essence, he asks the question, "Why me?" or "Why is this happening to me?"

The next chapters [3] are a series of speeches. A new address starts whenever the first verse of a chapter begins with "Person X said." These speeches, taken together, are a debate. The two sides in this debate are Job on one side, and his three friends on the other. The speakers alternate between Job on one side and the three friends on the other. Back and forth they go, each replying to the speech the other side just made, but also referring back to previous addresses made by themselves or the other participants.

The speeches themselves follow at least three rules. We don't know if this was normal or formal back then, but they seem to hold for this debate at least:

1. The two sides alternate their speeches.
2. The three participants on the one side speak each in his turn (probably the eldest first.)
3. They were to honor their opponent by presenting their argument as high-quality poetry.

However, despite the beautiful style with which they deliver their words, the words themselves are often anything but pleasant. The first six speeches by the three friends start with some variation on "you're an old windbag." Job resists responding in kind at first. But in about the

---

[3] Note that the chapter numbers were not in the original. So, some speeches take more than one chapter to deliver.

middle of the debate, he also says his accusers talk too much.

In a modern American political debate, the goal has almost become get in the best sound bite. Political debates are intended not to honor their opponent, but rather to destroy their opponent's arguments or character. And, if they're lucky, it destroys their opponent's candidacy as well. Facts seem to be merely side-issues; the goal is to demolish one's opponent. Hurting an opponent's feelings, or those of his/her supporters is part of the game of politics.

The debate format was close to the opposite for Job and his three friends. In this debate, the goal of the three friends is to help Job figure out what caused this horrific punishment. But they do so with style. Both sides present their arguments as high-quality poetry[4]. Their words may have been uncivilized, but the presentation of them was impressive.

Now we, the readers of Job, know from the prologue that Job's trials occurred not as punishment, but instead stem from a cosmic struggle between good and evil. But the debaters don't know about that part of the story at the time of the debate.

Their theological understandings almost certainly would prevent them from coming to any

---

[4] In English, the poetical structuring is not clear, because it doesn't have rhyme or meter. I do not know more than a smattering of Biblical Hebrew, but, many scholars have said that in Hebrew the poetry is magnificent and beautiful. It ranks high in the list of poetry from all time periods.

other conclusion than that God was punishing Job for some heinous sin. The punishments are ferocious, so the crime must have been equally bad.

Going further, even Job himself agrees with their position, at least at the beginning. He openly wonders what he could have done that could cause God to smite him so thoroughly. Much of his speeches' content is asking, "Why?"

Through the course of the speech-making, it becomes clear that the three friends believe Job must know what his sin was; after all, God would never punish someone like this unless the target knew the reason, right? Well, wrong, but they didn't know that. They assume that the calamities Job suffered *must* have been due to Job's sin. Further, it must have been a terrible sin, indeed. Job wouldn't be able to forget this sin, even if he could fool other people about it.

The debate ends with the three friends giving up in disgust because Job refuses to repent his terrible crime. (They don't say what crime, although they do take some wild guesses.) And, Job concludes his speeches with vows of exceptional commitment to following God's will thoroughly. He vows that his profession of innocence has always been real. The two sides are thus at an impasse.

ELIHU SPEAKS

But even though the primary debate is over, there is another present who has not spoken. Likely there were many onlookers, but there's at least one: we hear five speeches in succession from a young man named Elihu. Elihu has listened to all of the statements. And he puts his finger on two significant problems that they don't address.

But before he does, Elihu apologizes for speaking. He explains that even though he is younger than the other debaters, he still has some insight. He begs forgiveness for speaking, should they think he's out of line.

At the beginning of chapter 33, there's a break, but not for a new speech. It's more like (reading between the lines) someone tried to interrupt or respond, but Elihu wanted to keep speaking.

Whatever the pause meant, Elihu pushes forward as if it didn't happen. His second speech hits on the first issue he noticed: Elihu points out that the three friends have failed to articulate any actual sin that Job has committed. All they have done is make poor guesses. To compound their error, they have ignored Job's harsh questioning of God's will (and, thus, of God's character and wisdom.) Elihu tells them they're all terrible debaters; they brought up lots of things that didn't matter but missed the main issues completely.

I picture the scene as similar to an American teenager arguing with his parents. The other participants probably thought that way, too. After all, Elihu is very much younger than they are, and he isn't exactly kind.

But he must have hit a nerve because he is allowed to make a third speech (or second, depending on how you count them) when he points out that Job is questioning God's authority. After all, God ... is GOD, and it's not our place to question His actions, will, or anything else about Him. We live by faith, and that includes trusting that God's choices are correct and right. He correctly claims that Job has gone entirely overboard by *requiring* that God meet with him and discuss God's failings.

In his fourth speech, Elihu gets cranking: He points out that Job wants to challenge God's right to put Job through all this. Job wants a face-to-face meeting with God. Elihu points out that God is under no obligation to show up just to appease Job's desire for *justice*.

In the fifth and last of Elihu's speeches, he muses about God by comparing Him to a storm. Interestingly, at the end of his speech, God will speak "out of a storm" (Job 38:1, paraphrased.) Elihu may have been making his points using a real-life approaching storm as a metaphor. He would be pointing to it (as it gets closer and closer.) I sometimes wonder if they weren't getting a little uncomfortable in the face of this sandstorm, or worse.

Now, Elihu doesn't yet realize that the storm is God's vehicle or perhaps even God Himself. Elihu seems to be on the verge of saying that God isn't coming just for Job. That God is just too far above us to bother.

He *almost* says that.

But then, interrupting Elihu's speech, God arrives, speaking out of a whirlwind. He speaks with the full force of His formidable presence. He speaks from a storm as if to accentuate the fact that He is God, and to make sure that none of the hearers miss that little detail.

Never again, before or after, is it recorded that God spoke for this length of time to a human. Frequently when God shows up in person, people die. At a minimum, it changes them profoundly.

And what does He say? Readers might be hoping God will explain His actions. Doesn't Job at least deserve to know why? The answer is: apparently not. God starts with this:

> [1]Then the LORD answered Job out of the whirlwind and said, [2]"Who is this that darkens counsel by words without knowledge? [3]Now gird up your loins like a man, and I will ask you, and you instruct Me! [4]Where were you when I laid the foundation of the earth? Tell Me, if you have understanding, [5]Who set its measurements, since you know? Or Who stretched the line on it? [6]On what were its bases sunk? Or Who laid its cornerstone, [7]when the morning stars sang together and all the sons of God shouted for joy?" (Job 38:1-7)

From the first words out of His mouth, God clarifies that He has no intention of explaining His actions to Job. It seems obvious He doesn't plan on enlightening anybody else, either. (He *does* explain things, but not in a way they would *get* unless they spent some time pondering it.) Rarely do we find a better example of the adage, "God works in mysterious ways." We'll get to *why* he speaks this way later in this book.

He speaks, sometimes in rapid-fire questions, sometimes with longer prose. But *always* He speaks with one clear objective in mind: to put Job in his place. The questions He asks are unanswerable by Job. Many still are, even to this day.

God speaks for about 15 minutes, and then Job gets his first chance to reply. He essentially says, "I'm shutting up now." Job goes silent. His answer is similar to the modern teenager retort, "Whatever." Job wasn't apologizing or repenting. He is beaten, but not yet repentant.

That's not good enough for God. So in His next speech, God speaks of two of the most powerful creatures he ever created: the land-dwelling behemoth and the water-dwelling leviathan. While we don't know for sure what these creatures were, but we *do* know that God's description of their power brought Job from simply being silenced to being abjectly defeated, fully surrendering to God and repenting of his words. Those two descriptions to take Job from resignation to humility and repentance; Job must have known them to be fearsome creatures indeed!

THE EPILOGUE

Finally, God accepts this confession from Job (although, He doesn't *say* that to Job.)

Then He turns to the three friends and calls them liars. Specifically, He charges that they said untrue things about God, and they did so from a position of self-appointed authority. They had spoken of God as if they were God's messengers. And what they said was false.

I can imagine there's a bit of squirming going on at this point. Nobody we know of, since the days of Adam and Eve[5], had seen God this closely and survived. *Shaking in their boots* doesn't begin to describe it. They know full well what God should do: kill them outright. For their words had maligned the character and majesty of God.

Now seems like an ideal moment for a cartoon *lightning bolt* to fry them. Curiously, God does not kill them. Instead, He tells the three friends they should ask "My servant Job" (God's words) to offer a sacrifice for them and pray for them. This request will keep God from doing to them what their folly deserves. While God doesn't say which punishment He has in mind, it's clear it would not be a good thing.

God said they should have *Job* pray for them, and that God would accept Job's prayers on their behalf. So, the very man with whom they spent days or weeks arguing with, insulting by

---

[5] Technically, just after Cain kills Abel (Genesis 4.) But both Adam and Eve were alive then.

saying that he *must* have committed a heinous sin, and who they called names, that very man is the one to whom they must now humble themselves and ask to offer a sacrifice for them. The tables have turned. I think it's safe to declare, "the Lord works in mysterious ways."

Thus, because the three are required to go to Job for their very lives, it becomes evident that God has accepted Job's repentance!

Finally, restoration happens to Job. He gets ten more kids to replace the ten who died (we'll discuss the rather obvious problem of *replacing* kids later in the book.) His wealth doubles from what he had before, and he is entirely back in God's graces.

In addition to an overview of the book of Job, this chapter highlights two primary messages that show up throughout the book.

First, God is sovereign. Job needed to understand that *God ... Is GOD*, and Job, is not. Further, because this is true, Job (and we) must submit to God's will. Even when we do not understand or agree with God's plans, we must still accede to His Lordship in all things. He is always right because He is the very definition of *right*.

And second, the friends learned that one must never *assume* that that person's sin directly causes a calamity (that falls on that person). It may be, but it is never guaranteed (unless God says so), as they believed. Another way to say this is *Don't Blame the Victim*.

- God ... is God.
- Don't blame the victim.

Not as breathtaking as the view from an airplane, but still valuable.

1: THE GRINCH ... IN THE BIBLE?
(Job 1)

Dr. Seuss (Theodore Geisel) wrote a children's tale called How the Grinch Stole Christmas in 1957. Nine years later, the same story was told as a Christmas TV special by the same name.

It's a heartwarming story about a creature who hates Christmas (the Grinch), a town full of people who love Christmas (the Whos), and the Grinch's efforts to eradicate Christmas. The Grinch, disguised as Santa Claus, breaks into all the Whos' houses on Christmas Eve and steals all the presents, decorations, and Christmas food from the whole town. He's trying to steal Christmas itself, by taking the trappings that surround it.

The Grinch makes it clear he hates Christmas singing most of all. The Whos sing a Christmas carol of their own. After stealing all of the trappings of Christmas from the town, the Grinch is desperate to hear what he expects will be crying and sadness at the loss of Christmas.

But the Whos still sing their Christmas carol, totally befuddling the Grinch! In the end, he realizes that his theft of the trappings *of Christmas did not stop Christmas itself from coming. He has a change of heart and sleighs down into town to give the Whos back all of the stuff he stole.*

I can almost hear you thinking, how on earth does the story of a fictional green monster tell us anything about Job? Hang with me; I think it provides a neat analogy to the first half of the prologue.

At the beginning of Job, the book tells how excellent a person Job is. He worships and trusts God completely. Even God Himself says that Job is blameless and upright, implying that Job is unique on the earth in this respect. In my little parallel, Job's right way of living lines up with the Whos in Seuss' tale.

In my analogy, Christmas is Job's relationship with God, and the Grinch, of course, is Satan. He hates Job because he hates God, and Satan knows that God loves and is proud of Job.

But the parallel doesn't stop there. Satan believes that if he can destroy Job's life's trappings, Job will abandon God. Similarly to the Grinch, if he can remove the stuff, Job will give up on God.

What happens is that Job blesses God for his life, even after losing almost everything. It's a remarkable parallel to the Whos' continuing to celebrate Christmas, despite the Grinch's theft of all of the trappings of Christmas.

Satan couldn't destroy Job's relationship with God no matter what he did to Job.

Indeed, Job begins to get depressed when we get into his first speech. But his worship of God at the end of chapter one is even more worthy of tears of joy than is the Whos' maintaining Christmas in their hearts.

The illustration breaks down because, in chapter two, Satan harms Job himself, going where the Grinch story does not (the Grinch doesn't hurt the Whos themselves, just their stuff – hey, it's a children's story!)

Now, I hope you aren't thinking I'm trivializing Job's suffering by comparing it to a children's story. No, I intend to have us look at Job's tale differently than maybe we've done before. Throughout my book, I will ask questions that may be somewhat different from those you may have asked in the past about the same passages with which I'm dealing.

For example, please read this passage all the way through, without pausing, and aloud if you can. Pretend you are Job, listening to the four servants speak as they arrive (I've bolded the narrator's words to show the machinegun-like delivery):

> Now, on the day when his sons and his daughters were eating and drinking wine in their oldest brother's house, **a messenger came to Job and said,** "The oxen were plowing and the donkeys feeding beside them, and the Sabeans attacked and took them. They also slew the servants with the edge of the sword, and I alone have escaped to tell you."
>
> **While he was still speaking, another also came and said,** "The fire of God fell from heaven and burned up the sheep and the servants and consumed

them, and I alone have escaped to tell you."

While he was still speaking, another also came and said, "The Chaldeans formed three bands and made a raid on the camels and took them and slew the servants with the edge of the sword, and I alone have escaped to tell you."

While he was still speaking, another also came and said, "Your sons and your daughters were eating and drinking wine in their oldest brother's house, and behold, a great wind came from across the wilderness and struck the four corners of the house, and it fell on the young people, and they died, and I alone have escaped to tell you." (Job 1:13-19, bold emphasis mine)

The reason I asked you to read it aloud and without pausing is to get a sense of how things went for Job. Job didn't just lose his property and children, which would have been awful enough. No, he lost them in rapid-fire succession. Satan caused the calamities to happen with superbly evil timing. Job would hear of each tragedy immediately after he finished hearing about the previous. Four servants would tell Job of the near-complete loss of his wealth and the death of all 10 of his children. The bad news is all delivered within the space of a minute or two.

I've found that reading the calamities out loud and back-to-back makes Job's plight seem even more emotional than it already is. If readers haven't read the story before, some might not make it through in one pass. When I read this passage in my Sunday school classes on Job, there were usually one or two people who showed strong emotions as I read it.

Now, those classes were in a church where one would expect Bible knowledge to be relatively high. I didn't expect emotions to flow when I presented it this way the first time since it seemed likely they had read it before. But seeing the looks on some faces told me that it was emotional. More to the point, these people, who knew their Bible well, had never felt[6] it quite this way before.

Why? Because it puts us in Job's shoes. If you saw a movie about Job, and the movie crew portrayed the story well, it should cause emotional turmoil. Many times in this book, I'll be asking you to think as if if you were an actor in a movie. Try to put yourself into the mindset of the person in the story. For example, just after Job's heartbreaking lament, I ask the readers to pause and reflect: how would *I* respond to Job's sorrowful speech?

Job is a book for the ages. It has both powerful, thunderous messages to deliver, and yet also many easy-to-miss insights, hiding in plain sight, itching for discovery. I found that I must treat the story differently than most of the

---

[6] I used "felt" here, rather than "read", because, while they HAD read it before, they had not experienced it this way before.

other Bible books. Some of the juiciest tidbits only get noticed when one looks at passages from different angles.

The Grinch's tale is easy to understand. Even without mentioning Jesus, the story of the invulnerability of Christmas is straightforward. But have you ever thought about this part: a monster's redemption? After all, why was Jesus born? The name *Christmas* comes from Jesus's title, *Christ* (meaning redeemer or deliverer.)

> *If a children's story can have a deeper meaning, how much more so a tale God chose to include in His "living and active" eternal Bible[7]?*

---

[7] Hebrews 4:12 "For the word of God is living and active and sharper than any two-edged sword, and piercing as far as the division of soul and spirit, of both joints and marrow, and able to judge the thoughts and intentions of the heart."

2: SOME FUN WITH NUMBERS
(covering details in Job 1)

In the United States, it's almost a crime to be late for an appointment. And, people who live here think that this is one of the things that has brought about our greatness. When this author once visited Mexico, our host told us that the locals didn't treat time as rigidly as do those of us from the United States.

I still chuckle at the example Bill[8] gave. He said that if you had an appointment to pick your girlfriend up at 7 PM, and you came at 7:30, you would risk her still being in the shower.

Now, his point wasn't that we were somehow better. Far from it! He was simply telling how things worked; that time wasn't as critical as we might think it is.

Over the years, I've come across other people from other cultures, and I've begun to wonder if it isn't we Americans [9] who are *wrong* on this

---

[8] "Bill" was a missionary I visited during collegiate spring break in the 1970s. I don't have his permission to share this story (because I don't know how to contact him any more), so I'm leaving out his real name and details.

[9] I use "Americans" rather loosely here. In fact, Canadians, Mexicans, Chileans, and Brazilians are just as much Americans as those of us in the US. But, it's so much easier to read than "people from the United States of America", or even worse "United Statesians", so I hope you'll

subject. Even in the church, being punctual is somehow considered a virtue, and tardiness is almost a sin.

But where is that in Scripture? I've looked for it and asked others, but nobody yet has pointed out a place where punctuality is of much concern at all, let alone a virtue.

In Job, many statements appear, some of which are arguably imprecise. At the beginning of the book, it says that he had "7000 sheep, 3000 camels, 500 yoke of oxen, 500 female donkeys, and many servants." But did he really have precisely 7000 sheep, and not 7001 or 6999?

To many Americans, these are imprecise (and thus, *false*) numbers. He most likely did not have precisely 7000 sheep, and to say he did is *wrong*.

Unfortunately, that's just pride speaking. To be sure, even professional scientists are continuously estimating things. A scientist might say that the value of pi is 3.14. S/he knows it's not *precisely* 3.14, but s/he also knows that nobody wants to read an infinite string of numbers just to be accurate. We consider sunset or sunrise to happen in a specific hour and minute of the day, but it occurs at an exact point in time. The period sunrise (and sunset) occur over is infinitely closer to zero than it is to even a second. Yet we're OK with estimating that.

I bring this up not to accuse us of jingoism, but rather because we're going to have to step

---

suffer a little inaccuracy without offense, should you not reside in the United States.

outside of our cultural biases quite a few times while burrowing through Job. We must resist the urge to dismiss a comment simply because it's not accurate enough or precise enough. I'll be pointing these out as we go through the book. I do this because sometimes we miss points unless we set aside cultural blinders.

This book was written, in my opinion, almost 4000 years ago (around the time of Abraham, a few hundred years after Noah's flood), and the lifestyles back then might be considered strange now. One reason we don't know an exact date for the book of Job is because it wasn't vital for them to record that back then.

We also don't know who wrote the book. The author could have chosen not to record his/her name as a cultural thing or a modesty issue. I believe Job wrote it, and that he did so reflecting upon what he had learned. Such an important subject might very well cause even the most outgoing among us to shy away from putting our name on it.

Was it *wrong* for the author not to include his name? Is it wrong to not be able to date the book precisely? You can be the judge, but like approximating numbers, I won't be too dogmatic about it. This book calls for flexibility in several areas. Several times in my musings, I'll point out that our modern or American mentality clouds our perspective.

See? A whole chapter on numbers and you didn't even get bored (I hope!)

3: MISERY DOES NOT LOVE COMPANY

(Job 2 - 3)

In Disney's Aladdin, Genie describes the restrictions on what Aladdin is allowed to wish. One of the limits is that Genie cannot kill people. In the sequel, the evil genie says, mockingly, "you'd be surprised what you can live through." Later, it appears that the evil genie has killed Iago. The evil genie blasted Iago, and he looks dead. But, singed and still alive, Iago scratches out, "you'd be surprised what you can live through." And everybody is happy again.

The book of Job continues with more of the same from Satan. He doesn't admit he lost the bet with God, and he pulls a childish "how about best two out of three?" Satan claims that God rigged the game by not letting Satan touch the man himself, but only his stuff. (As if losing ten children at one time doesn't count.)

When I look at Satan here, I see a spoiled brat who didn't get his or her way. But in a curious twist, God grants Satan's second request. He says Satan can harm, but not kill, Job.

If we thought that the rapid-fire list of staggering calamities in the first half (of Satan's attacks) was terrible, think about just how sick Satan could make someone, even if prevented from causing death. And, so he does.

Job is stricken with a disease that caused painful boils. Job would scratch them with pottery shards, to relieve the itchiness and the pain. Yet Satan does his job well: the itching and suffering continue, despite Job's best efforts at getting relief.

Like Genie, Satan is not allowed to kill Job. But he *can* make continued living dismal. Job's skin might look a lot like Iago's singed feathers. Unfortunately, this tale is all-too-true.

Even Job's wife thinks Job should give up. She says, "Do you still hold fast your integrity? Curse God and die!" Job refuses. He's hurt, but he will not sin, even to end the struggle.

Job then sits down on the road, throwing dust and ashes on himself. This practice was a sign of total despair in the days of the ancients. Anybody who looked at someone doing this would know that something awful had happened to him. For example, losing a child or job could cause this kind of grief. (Never mind that Job lost both, and not just one child, but all ten.)

Some time passes, and then three of Job's friends arrive to comfort him. From a distance, they can't even tell who he is because of the disease. Remember, Job is scratching his boils, which is causing them to leak fluids. Then, he's been throwing road dust and ashes on himself. It's hard to imagine just how poorly Job appeared.

The three friends give us a significant clue: they sit on the road with Job, and *none* of them speaks a word for a whole week. Indeed, his condition is heartbreaking.

After a week with all four of them sitting silently, Job speaks. He offers a sad lament about his life. He curses the day he was born. He curses the knowledge that a son had been born to his parents. He asks that God make it as if it never happened. He would like his birthday stricken from the calendar.

In a curious twist, he asks men who prepare to rouse Leviathan to curse that day. Now, men who would qualify to rouse Leviathan are few and far between. Perhaps some action hero from the movies would try, but real people? If Leviathan existed today, it's not likely anybody would try tackling it even with modern hunting weapons. So it's a cinch nobody would attempt it with the primitive weapons available at the time.

The twist is that God will refer to Leviathan as His final argument against Job's challenge of God's authority. Leviathan (and Behemoth) are the last straws that break the camel's back of Job. They are God's *piece de resistance* of His arguments. Leviathan is one of two creatures whose might and fearsome presence finally convince Job to repent fully. Leviathan is a singularly ferocious creature. It seems probable that God remembered Job speaking of this creature, and that He used it to finally humble Job.

But back to this speech, beyond just cursing the day of his birth, Job also asks that his mother never existed. Or that he had been born stillborn. Or perhaps a miscarriage. Then, at least, he might be at peace.

He wonders why God still allows the sun to shine on him. He laments his life and desires his death. Worse, he is fearful that God is not done with him yet.

Honestly, this kind of misery does not enjoy company. My trials pale in comparison to Job's. But even those events caused me to want to be alone more often than not. I have at least a shadow of an idea as to how hurt Job's heart is. And, I suspect you might, too.

But at least his friends have come to comfort him, have they not? *(Like Iago's friends did?)*

Well, maybe not:

4: THE "SPANISH INQUISITION"
(Job 4 - 5)

Monty Python is famous for many comedic things, but one of the better ones is about the Spanish Inquisition[10]. Some innocuous person is answering questions peppered at him from another person. As the questions keep coming, he frustratingly exclaims, "I wasn't expecting a kind of Spanish Inquisition."

Immediately some men in pious red robes enter the room, saying, "<u>Nobody expects the Spanish Inquisition. Our chief weapon is surprise. Surprise and fear. ... Our TWO weapons are surprise and fear and ruthlessness.</u>" He continues, adding a new item to the list each time, and revising the count as he goes along.

Not to be outdone, it's time for us to do a little role-playing. But not in a comedic fashion: After reading about Job's plight and seeing his lamentation speech, what's your reaction?

For me, the first time I read it, I felt sorry for the guy. The disasters that hit Job were just terrible, the worst I had ever heard about, outside of what Jesus suffered. Now, God planned Jesus's trials, and Jesus knew all about them. He willingly jumped into the agony He endured.

---

[10] Monty Python's Flying Circus, season 2, episode 15.

But Job did not jump into these trials willingly; God didn't even ask[11]. Job had no say in what happened to him. All he knew was that he had lived his life as near to God's designs as he knew how. And, as we found out in Job 1, God agreed with Job: Job *had indeed* lived uprightly.

Both Job and his three friends labored under a huge misconception: simplified, they believed that calamity is always a punishment. We'll cover this more later, but for now, it's essential to realize that Job agrees with his detractors: he thinks he has done *something* to deserve his fate.

During that week of silence at the end of Job 2, Job no doubt tried to think of what it was that he had done. But he could come up with nothing. At that point, he is probably eager to hear what his friends have to say.

> [1]Then Eliphaz the Temanite answered,
> [2]"If one ventures a word with you, will you become impatient? But who can refrain from speaking?"

WHAT???

He's asking Job if he will get upset should Eliphaz speak. That's a polite way of saying, "shut up and listen." Or, perhaps, he's just introducing us to the Sumerian [12] Inquisition? Eliphaz has

---

[11] There will be more on this issue at the end of this book.

[12] Sumeria was an ancient kingdom that may have been the dominant civilization near where Job lived.

concluded that he knows what Job's root problem is, and he's about to tell the audience. These are not comforting words, at least not how I define comforting.

Then he launches into a little buttering up, telling Job that Job's words have, in the past, helped the weak. But now it is Job who needs help. OK, that's not so bad, except that the real meaning is being couched in polite words, as we're about to find out.

He then asks whether Job trusts God or not. This statement is an apparent attack; the meaning can't be more explicit. Even so, he outright says it: the innocent do not get punished like this.

He's sort of right, but for all the wrong reasons. Yes, God doesn't punish innocent[13]. But, it isn't punishment. Calamity has overtaken Job. There's a huge difference. We'll cover this in more detail later, but the critical thought, for now, is that this is not punishment. Even so, all of the debate participants seem to believe that it is punishment.

Eliphaz has delivered the opening salvo in his first speech. The attacks are veiled and not very severe. But they are attacks nonetheless, and Job will respond to them in Job 6 when Job takes his turn speaking in the debate.

What I most want to focus on in Eliphaz's first speech (Job 4 & 5) is the source. Take a look at this section:

---

[13] The "innocent" are never punished, because there are no innocent people. But, that's a side issue here.

¹²Now, a word was brought to me stealthily, and my ear received a whisper of it. ¹³Amid disquieting thoughts from the visions of the night, when deep sleep falls on men, ¹⁴dread came upon me, and trembling, and made all my bones shake. ¹⁵Then a spirit passed by my face; the hair of my flesh bristled up. ¹⁶It stood still, but I could not discern its appearance; a form was before my eyes; there was silence, then I heard a voice: ¹⁷"Can mankind be just before God? Can a man be pure before his Maker? ¹⁸He puts no trust even in His servants, and against His angels He charges error. ¹⁹How much more those who dwell in houses of clay, whose foundation is in the dust, who are crushed before the moth! ²⁰Between morning and evening, they are broken in pieces; unobserved, they perish forever. ²¹Is not their tent-cord plucked up within them? They die, yet without wisdom." Job 4:12-21

There are a few things of note here that can give us clues as to the identity of this spirit. Spirits are from outside of the realm in which we live. And, there are two kinds of spirits: good and evil. Can we figure out who *this* spirit is?

Verse 12 gives the first clue in this passage: the message came stealthily. Now, it is true that God sometimes speaks softly, sometimes even in a whisper [14]. But this message came stealthily. The Hebrew word means stolen, or stolen away; God does not talk this way. So, we can rule out God and, by extension, his obedient angels.

The next clue (verse 13) is that the words came with disquieting thoughts at night. God's words either strike terror into the hearts of the hearers, or they are comforting beyond measure. When God speaks, it's never merely unsettling. So again, God gets ruled out as the messenger.

Plus, God speaks plainly, usually during the day. He does send dreams and visions at night, though.

In verse 14, Eliphaz is terrified. Now, God is indeed a terrifying presence. But one of two things always happens when He appears in this manner. Either the person gets a statement of judgment, or the person hears "fear not." Neither of those two happens here; Eliphaz is allowed to be fearful. So again, we can rule God out of the possibilities.

You may have noted that none of the clues rules out Satan. And, we already know, from chapter one, that Satan has a vested interest in tormenting Job. So, he could be the whisperer Eliphaz heard. Let's look further into that idea.

A spirit passes by Eliphaz's face (verse 15.) It causes the hair of his flesh to stand up. A reaction like this doesn't ever get attributed to God, but Satan certainly fits the description. I

---

[14] In 1 Kings 19:11-13, God speaks from a gentle breeze.

think we may be getting closer to understanding from where this message came.

Finally, the message itself provides the final clue: "Can mankind be just before God?" This message is from the accuser himself, Satan. His job is to indict humanity; his name, in Hebrew, means accuser.

But he overexposes himself if he was trying to hide who spoke. Pity Eliphaz didn't notice that he says "against His angels He charges error." Satan is no longer an angel, nor are his disobedient minions, the demons. So, this is patently false. Of course, Satan is a liar and the father of lies (John 8:44), so saying something like this follows right along with Satan's fundamental nature.

So, now we know the source: the message comes from the forces of darkness[15]. By that, I mean either Satan himself or one (or more) of his fallen-angels, demons.

I think we can further narrow down the culprit by noting that Satan wants these speeches (by Eliphaz and the other two friends) to cause Job to sin. It's vital to him, so it seems unlikely that he would entrust it to a mere demon, even a high-ranking (one if such creatures have ranks). Thus, I conclude that it is likely that Satan himself (and not one of his minions) is the one who delivered the message.

Eliphaz says more, but the bottom line is that he thinks Job has committed some heinous

---

[15] However, it doesn't have to be Satan himself, at this point in the argument.

sin, and he wants Job to turn from his wicked ways and back to God.

> *Even Monty Python couldn't make this funny.*

But Satan isn't the one to blame for the creation of Eliphaz's speech. Another reason is much more down-to-earth:

5: BAD THINGS, GOOD PEOPLE?
(Job 4 – 5, again)

In the late 1800s, the Brown family of Exeter, Rhode Island, seemed cursed. George Brown lost his wife Mary, his daughter Mary, and his other daughter, Mercy. They all died of what they called Consumption. *The family just seemed cursed. When George Brown's only remaining child, Edwin, also got sick, the townsfolk knew what the problem was: One of wife Mary, daughter Mary, or Mercy Brown was sucking the life out of the remaining family members, from the grave. They thought one of the three women was undead.*

After convincing a reluctant George, the locals exhumed the bodies. Mercy's body looked in excellent condition, barely decayed at all. This state of non-decay was the final nail in the coffin, so to speak: she obviously (to the townsfolk) had become what today we would call a vampire. Equally apparent to them is the solution: burn Mercy's heart and have Edwin consume the ashes.

They did, and Edwin consumed it, but he died anyhow.

Today we know that what took the four lives (and many others in the area) was Tuberculosis. Preservation occurred not because she was undead, but simply because they stored her body in an above-ground crypt in a New England winter. They could not bury her because it was too cold to dig a grave. The vault left her body completely frozen, virtually untouched by decay.

This tale, which may be one of the inspirations for Bram Stoker's *Dracula*, is an example of falsely attributing a calamity as a punishment or curse. The author wrote Job's sad tale with at least one clear purpose: to teach us that we should never assume that the victim's sin caused the calamity that hits a person. Poor Edwin should never have had to consume his dead sister's heart.

Throughout history, people have claimed that calamities come from deities or curses. Witch trials, some claims of heresy, and even wars have occurred because people falsely assumed that the cause of the catastrophe was something done by the person or people the tragedy hit. People have attributed natural disasters like tsunamis and hurricanes to the sinful lifestyles of those living in the areas hit. This attribution has happened as recently as this 21st century. (We haven't progressed much in 4000 years, have we?)

In Job, God Himself declares Job blameless and upright. As far as God is concerned, Job is sinless. Now, if the all-knowing God of the universe cannot come up with something Job has done wrong, then it seems to this author's "little grey cells" [16] that Job has indeed not done anything wrong.

---

[16] Quoted from, and with apologies to, Agatha Christie's famous detective Hercule Poirot.

To be sure, guilty people almost always deny their guilt. So, to a degree, we can understand why his three friends are skeptical. But once Job staunchly maintains his innocence, shouldn't a true friend just believe him and try to comfort him truly?

But instead, Eliphaz, Bildad, and Zophar turn their language more acidic as the debate goes on. They are confident that Job has sinned, and that he has sinned heinously. It's *obvious* from Job's punishment: Job is guilty of doing something very wrong. Their side of the debate takes it upon themselves not to see *if* Job is guilty, but rather what specific sins Job has committed? Over and over again, they re-ask the same question using different words: "What have you done, Job?"

In contrast, Elihu notices (starting in Job 33) that the three friends ultimately failed to find out what the sin was. He calls to the carpet the three friends (who are his elders and thus should know better.) He chastises them for not figuring out Job's sin, and yet still maligning Job.

Even when God speaks, He does not explain any sin that caused these trials. He questions Job severely, but it's for trusting God with only 99%, not because of some evil thing Job has done.

So, in the end, there is nobody to accuse Job. What, then, are we to conclude? For the answer to that, we have to dig deeper; we must ask more questions.

The first question is, "Why is this story important?" We know it *is* essential because God placed it in the Bible. God's Word will exist forever, but it is limited in size. To put a story of this size there, God must have had some excellent reasons.

Further, God allowed his most faithful servant of that time [17] to undergo horrific calamities, worse than any other recorded human. Again, God must have had excellent reasons, indeed!

Our God is awesome; there are many reasons. But one specific reason regarding this story is to show people who will listen that calamities do not necessarily mean the victim sinned. In other words, we cannot assume that disasters that strike a person (or a nation) happen because of that person's (or nation's) direct actions.

Yes, God has caused calamities. He has wiped nations from existence. He sent his people into exile three times[18] for defying Him.

However, when God causes a calamity for a purpose, He always says so. He states it to that person or nation or another person or involved country that may be watching. For example, the kingdom of Babylon, into which Judah went into captivity, would be punished by destruction. So

---

[17] Noah, Job, and Daniel are singled out by God as being three who could save themselves ... only ... from the calamity God was about to send on Jerusalem. (Ezekiel 14:14, 20.) So, it's quite possible that Job was one of the four most righteous people in history (Jesus being the fourth.)

[18] In 722 BC God sent the northern kingdom of Israel into exile. In 586 BC, God sent the southern kingdom of Judah into exile. And in 70 AD, God sent the whole nation into exile for rejecting their Messiah, Jesus.

comprehensive that no town would ever arise there again. (It's an uninhabitable swamp now.)

Many times God judges nations or people and sends calamities to correct or punish them. He does so for different reasons, but He always states His logic.

So, what about calamities that God did not explain? To my knowledge, God made no statements about Hurricane Katrina or the 2004 tsunami. But that didn't stop some people[19] from claiming that, to them, it was apparent the damage was punishment for their sin.

Obvious as it may seem to them or us, we simply should not make such an assumption. Job's tale tells us clearly that God does not *just* send calamities as punishment. We simply cannot blame the victim unless God says so.

So, why *does* He allow calamity, if He did not directly send it? In other words, "Why do bad things happen to good people?"

The answer is that we live in a sin-cursed world. Adam and Eve were real people who sinned against God in Genesis 3. The punishment became hard labor, pain, and a death sentence. The Hebrew for "you shall surely die" in Genesis 2:17 is the same word used twice. The first use of dying is an infinitive (signifying ongoing action, or "dying" in English). The infinitive verb is followed by an imperfect (meaning an act which has not yet been completed, or "shall die" in English)[20]. A

---

[19] I will not mention names, because that could denigrate their otherwise good names.

[20] Genesis 2:17 from www.BlueLetterBible.org

good translation, albeit stilted, would be "dying, you will die."

In other words, they would die a death that would continue their dying forever.

Also, God cursed the universe along with Adam and Eve because God had given creation to them. When Adam chose to sin, he caused the Earth to begin the process of dying, just as Adam himself was now dying. According to Paul in Romans 8:22, "The whole creation groans and suffers the pains of childbirth."

Part of that corruption or curse is that the world is falling apart.

People often ask the question, "Why do bad things happen to good people?" Here we have the answer: because we and indeed the whole universe are suffering under a curse almost as old as time. The sin of manKIND causes most calamities, not the sin of individual people or even nations. So, bad things happen, period. It doesn't matter whether we're good or bad; both bad and good things will happen to us. This answer covers the first thought in the quote, "Why do bad things happen to good people?": Mankind's sin causes calamities.

To answer the rest of the question, we *all* sin! We continue to sin, thus confirming that God was right to curse us and sentence us to death. Indeed, none of us are in any way *good*. Bad things don't happen to good people because *there are no good people!* (Mark 10:18 and Luke 18:19; in Jesus' own words, "No one is good except God alone.")

Indeed, the real question we should ask is, "Why does God allow anything *good* to happen to us?" We do not deserve anything positive from Him, and yet God gives us good things.

Why? God is merciful, and He loves us. He gives us good things even though we don't deserve it. And, difficult as it may be to hear, one of those good things is what happened to Job.

It wasn't favorable for Job in the usual sense. Sure, Job grew into a deeper relationship with God as a result. But the trials were horrendous, not what one would call good.

True, but it *is* good … for us! One reason is that, if we have realized the message, it forces us to own up to our tendency to say "s/he deserved that" about bad things when they happen to others.

We sometimes do this to ourselves as well. One of the most challenging tasks psychologists can run into is convincing an abuse victim that s/he did not deserve what happened to him/her. From my personal experience with some abused friends, it can take years to overcome the despair of believing that they themselves caused the harm forced upon them. They were powerless, and yet they blamed themselves.

A key message from Job is that we cannot assume that calamity equals punishment for individual sin, including our own. The sole exception is when God says it is. And, this message, in particular, is practically shouted at us: the three friends were called to the carpet by God Himself on the subject.

Would that we do not follow in their path.

Unlike Mercy Brown, Job isn't dead. He hopes for answers through his friends' words.

6: WE'RE TALKING ABOUT GOD!
(Job 6 - 7)

At the end of Empire Strikes Back, *when it appears all is lost, the camera turns to Yoda. Yoda, through the Force, has learned that Darth Vader has defeated Luke, and his countenance droops at the realization.*

Job's reaction is similar. He feels defeated. At first, Job does not even speak to Eliphaz's argument. No, instead he is recapping his grief and pain in the first half of the chapter.

For example, in verses 2-3, he makes a word picture for them: if a scale could weigh his grief, it would be burdensome. It's his way of telling his friends that they just don't understand.

Job claims that God has fiercely attacked him. It almost seems like he's asking, "why can't you understand?"? I suspect his tone of voice would have conveyed something like that, but we can't be sure. But it sure fits with the tenor of the passage.

First, he points out that when an animal is hungry, the animal may "speak" (like a donkey braying or our pet rabbit Samwise scratching at his canister of food at 8:30 every evening.) But he says that when an animal does this, it gets little attention. However, Job has complained in deep anguish, and for obviously good reasons. Yet he has been chastised for doing so.

Here he just begs God to "get it over with!" He, along with his friends, likely holds to theology that when God punishes severely (which Job's trials seem to be), the result will be death. It goes along with the stance that we get recompensed in this life for our deeds.

So, Job believes that God is just building up to his eventual death. Here he merely wishes for that end to arrive; he wants no more pain.

Even so, Job rejoices: "But it is still my consolation, and I rejoice in unsparing pain, that I have not denied the words of the Holy One" (Job 6:10). He trusts not in strength (which he doesn't have anyway) or his armor-plated skin (which he also doesn't have.) He knows that he does not have it in himself to win this battle.

Finally, starting in verse 14, he gets around to responding to Eliphaz. He expected compassion and kindness from his friends. Instead, he received a *wadi*. A wadi is a seasonal pool or stream in a desert, which disappears, leaving behind only dry land, but with enough contours to remind the unlucky traveler that there *was* a pool or creek there. The most important thing about wadis, and the main point of Job using the metaphor, is that they're unreliable.

Job had hoped his friends would empathize with him, or even just sympathized with him. But instead, they attacked. He would have liked a glass of fresh water, but instead was given a dried-up stream.

He follows up his thoughts about wadis by rhetorically asking if he had asked for a bribe or something. He knows he didn't, but just in case, he's asking for proof.

He now openly demands that the others show him his sin, which caused him to deserve the punishment he has received. This request is eerily similar to Jesus asking his opponents which one of them could point out His sin. The answer, known fully to Job and Jesus, is the same: there isn't any.

In other words, "put up or shut up!"

Down in verse 25, Job blasts Eliphaz's response: "How painful are honest words! But what does your argument prove?" Job is openly stating that he wants them to show him whatever sin it was that he is supposed to have committed. This statement is not a metaphor or an insult. It's a from-the-heart statement asking for them to point out his sin. Job honestly does not know why this is happening, and he's asking (begging, really) for his friends to help him find the crime. After all, we're human; thus, we even forget sins.

We know the truth, the truth that Job suspects: there *is* no sin. His trials are not punishment, despite how it appears. But even Job cannot accept this wholeheartedly. His theological underpinnings tell him that this is punishment, and therefore he must have done something wrong. It's only logical.

As we move forward in the book, an odd twist will become apparent. As Job's friends get more belligerent and forceful in their pronouncements that Job has sinned dramatically, Job himself will become more and more convinced of his innocence. And that leads to his only manifest sin in the whole book:

challenging God's right to govern the universe His way. We'll have more on this later.

Now might be a good time to remember what Job has gone through, and *why* he used the words he used. He lost almost all his material wealth and all ten of his children. It took mere minutes to tell him of *all* of these losses. Then, as if that weren't enough, he later lost his health. Not like he got cancer or anything like that, where at least there will be the finality of death. No, to him, this is worse, for he fears that the incredibly painful illness he is suffering will last a very long time, with no relief.

No, Eliphaz proved nothing with his argument. And thus, Job gets angry. He implies his friends would gamble for orphans and barter for a friend. Then he gets personal: "Look at my face. Am I lying to you?" (Job 6:26-30, my paraphrase)

He intended that rhetorically since they're already looking at him. Indeed, it has a clear implied answer: no, he's not lying. So, he demands that they stop, for his words are right, and his conscience is clear.

Finished with Eliphaz' lame argument, in chapter 7, he returns to lamenting his life by noting how difficult life is, wasted away waiting for his wages: months of vanity. Yoda at least had some hope. Job can see none.

When Job goes to bed, he longs to rise again because of his great night pains. He sees skin covered with scabs and oozing fluids, all at the same time.

At the time I am writing this, I have a sore back. It keeps waking me up at night. I want to sleep, but sleep is fleeting. I think Job is experiencing something similar. Now I know that I'll eventually get better. Job laments how he expects never to recover.

At this point, it might be useful to remind ourselves of Job's restoration at the end of the book. It's been getting pretty depressing, so please keep the end in mind as you read on.

Then he speaks of the grave. He feels that this is his destiny and that it's just a matter of time. Further, once he does die, there's nothing more after that. He is incorrect, but remember his and his friends' flawed theology: this life is pretty much all there is. Later in the book, we'll see hopeful words that imply he didn't *fully* believe there was no life after this one. But for now, his hopelessness prevails, and he doesn't question the theological underpinnings.

But then he erupts. After all his depressing thoughts and speech, he claims that he will boldly continue to make his statements! He's saying, What's the worst that can happen?

Then there's a significant shift. In Job 7:12 (and to the end of chapter 7), Job primarily addresses God, not his friends. Here he notes that God seems to be hovering over Job, watching every move, and waiting to pounce. While God *is* watching over him, it's not because He is not waiting to pounce. He's waiting until the debate is over; then He will have *His* say in the matter.

Back to Job's thoughts: Job thinks God is watching like a hawk eyeing prey. If Job tries to sleep, he has nightmares. He asks God to leave him alone.

Time for another reminder for readers: *God* didn't give him disease, nightmares, and pain. Satan did. But God *allowed* these things. But since God is sovereign and did *allow* all this, We can think of God as the cause.

However, Job can't see all that. He doesn't know there is an enemy of our souls trying to harm us at every turn, and even more so if we follow God!

So, he agrees with his friends' fundamental theology: he has indeed done something wrong. But he does not know what that sin is.

Job somberly states his plight. Like Yoda, Job's countenance also has fallen.

7: BE COMFORTED
(Job 8)

In the movie Hunt for Red October, *the captain tells Jack to be careful in the next room because "some things in here don't react well to bullets." It turns out it's the room where the nuclear missiles are stored.*

Jack is careful, but the KGB agent he's chasing fires his gun many times. Jack's response is, "and he says I have to be careful?"

In his just-finished speech, Job asked his friends to be considerate of him, since he's already wounded. But like the KGB agent, Bildad the Shuhite[21] doesn't let that bother him. He is a man of fewer words than Eliphaz, but he seems more robust than Eliphaz in harshness.

Bildad starts with, "How long will you say these things, and the words of your mouth be a mighty wind" (Job 8:2)? When Eliphaz began, he didn't directly insult Job. He beat around the bush a bit: "If one ventures a word with you, will you become impatient? But who can refrain from speaking" (Job 4:2)? Bildad comes right out and speaks his mind, saying in effect, "how long are you going to talk, windbag?" It seems the gloves are off.

---

[21] Please, no jokes about him being the shortest guy in the Bible; it's spelled Shuhite, not shoe-height.

Remember, though, that he probably thinks he is defending God against Job's rash words. As we'll find out at the end of the story, God doesn't need help defending Himself. And, He certainly isn't looking for someone to speak falsehoods on His *behalf*.

He asks a straightforward question, "Does God pervert justice?" There is truth in what he says: God certainly does *not* pervert justice. To do so would be to deny His nature. So, that much is true.

But *why* is Bildad asking this question? He points out that God wouldn't kill Job's children, except for *their* sins. (He's going to go further later and claim that Job's kids died for Job's sin as well.)

Now, put yourself into Bildad's shoes. Would you speak like this to a man who just lost everything? Or into Job's shoes: what would you feel if you were in Job's situation and Bildad spoke such things?

I know I (as Job) wouldn't respond very gracefully at this point. It's one thing to pick on Job himself, but to attack his children, all of whom are dead now? This attack is probably one reason why God chose Job to go through this set of trials: he could speak in much more measured tones and words than most people.

In verse 5, Bildad dares to imply that he *knows* that Job has sinned. Now, if this were a mystery novel, there might be something hidden from the reader. But it's not; we were told at the beginning of the book, by God Himself, that Job is "blameless and upright." And, Satan implicitly accepted this judgment, or he wouldn't need to test Job's character; he would already have enough to hang Job at that point!

But here, Bildad blatantly states that Job has sinned, and his sons have sinned, and that's the reason for the punishment levied upon him. He even goes so far as to state that, if Job repented, restoration would happen. Of course, that can't include Job's children, but Bildad isn't interested in the full truth.

God has never promised to restore individual sinners' wealth if they repent. He will later, many times during Israel's turbulent history. But to this point in history, God has said no such thing. He hasn't even promised to forgive sin at all[22].

Next, he asks Job to learn from history. Remember what your dad taught you. And your grandpa. And Noah and other Godly people. Bildad says they will agree with him. I'm not exactly sure how he knows that since he has likely been alive a shorter time than Job or Eliphaz[23]. Still, this is what he believes.

In any event, I'm glad God shows up at the end of this book and sets the record straight.

---

[22] He actually has, but not clearly. Animal sacrifices can't remove sin; they merely cover it up (see the book of Hebrews, especially chapter 9.) So, when God killed a sheep to give coverings to Adam and Eve, he was covering over their sin in addition to their bodies. But, that's not stated in the Bible until the time of Moses.

[23] It's possible that Noah is still alive when the events in Job took place. So, Bildad may have intended for Job to contact Noah. However, this is a long-shot. Even the most aggressive "date it very old" people still have it occurring in Abraham's time, which is after Noah died.

Otherwise, some people might think the three friends had it right. But no, God dismisses their words as folly and adds a command to them to ask Job to pray for them. Payback *is* coming, folks.

Then he wanders in his thinking a bit, giving Job a history lesson, an agronomy lesson, and an entomology lesson as if he is trying to make up his mind what to say. Recall that most of Eliphaz's speech was probably written down in advance, only wordsmithed somewhat to account for Job's statements. However, Bildad, while he probably had a prepared speech, had to change it significantly more, since Job has spoken twice now, and Eliphaz once.

Ultimately, Bildad makes the baseless claim that if Job merely repents, God will restore him. But since Job has *not* repented, he will suffer a two-edged judgment. First, he sarcastically says that there's a joy that Job won't feel. But there's a second joy that other people around Job *will* feel.

The bottom line in Bildad's speech is that Job is *not* righteous, and God is punishing him. These are pretty bold claims to make. And, to top it off, he presented absolutely no evidence of Job's so-called sin. No wonder God includes him when He demands a sacrifice at the end of the book.

The KGB agent continued firing. So will Bildad.

8: WITH FRIENDS LIKE THIS...
(Job 9)

In 1939, Germany and the Soviet Union signed a pact of mutual non-aggression. In effect, they became friends. *Now, neither Hitler nor Stalin believed for a minute that the other was a* friend *(Hitler hated communism even more than he disdained democracy. It was more of a pact of mutual "I don't feel like bothering with you for now."*

Hitler would break the pact in 1942. At that point, I can imagine Stalin saying something like a Russian version of "With friends like this, who needs enemies?"

Something similar is happening in Job. His friends are proving to be anything *but* friends.

But in Job's response to Bildad, a scary thing happens: Job begins the speech by saying that Bildad is right.

Now, hold on a minute; haven't I been saying that they are wrong? That even God says, they're wrong? Is the Bible contradicting itself?

No, it's not. *Job* says that Bildad is right, not God. While interpreting Scripture, we need to be careful to avoid the trap of assigning truth to statements that are merely quotations. Only when it is God or His agent speaking do we know it is biblical truth.

Job will be proven wrong by the events of the book that bears his name. He's holding to lousy theology. But the Bible accurately records even false statements.

Romans 3:23 ("all have sinned and fall short of the glory of God.") agrees with them when understood rigidly. But it's wrong to read it that way. All cannot mean "every person who ever lived," because Jesus is a person, and He never sinned. There can be God-ordained exceptions.

God Himself declared Job righteous to the great accuser, Satan. If Job had sinned as Romans 3:23 implies, indeed Satan would have just said so, instead of having to put him through a test.

Somehow, Job was considered righteous. That doesn't happen through being good or doing good works, folks. It only happens through a relationship with God based on faith. Jesus paid the price for all people, including Job [24]. Job's sacrifices were just Job's way of maintaining a healthy relationship with God. His sacrifices and righteousness came from his believing heart, not from a list of dos and don'ts. This situation is similar to Abraham's, whose trust in God was reckoned as righteousness (see Genesis 15:6 and Galatians 3:6.)

Now we get to the real problem: Job's friends are openly stating what Job fears has

---

[24] This is the full meaning of Romans 3:23, mentioned in the previous paragraphs: we all need a Savior. It's not meant to be a precise statement of the lives of every person. Job still needs a Savior, like everybody else. After all, the sacrifices he has made throughout his life do not remove sin; they merely put the day of reckoning off into the future, when Jesus' sacrifice would make it official. God can call Job blameless because He is not limited by time, as we are. To Him, Jesus' death had effectively already happened.

happened: God has withdrawn His friendship with Job.

The friends think they *know* this is true. Job even agrees that it must be true. But the difference is that the friends say Job *does* know why this has happened, and Job says he does not know. Ultimately, the real answer is that it has nothing to do with any sin Job might or might not have committed. It's a test of Job's relationship with God (although Satan sees it differently.)

Job says, "If one wished to dispute with Him, he could not answer Him once in a thousand times" (Job 9:3). Thus, Job *knows* that he has no right to demand an answer from God. Yet he spends most of his speeches doing precisely that.

All of creation testifies to God's power. A man has nothing to compare. From a legal perspective, people do not have standing, *i.e.*, the legal right to challenge.

So, all of that is true: Job doesn't have the right to challenge God's actions. Since he does this repeatedly in his speeches, this is the only *sin* of which Job is guilty: declaring God wrong.

The problem is that God is so *so* far above us that we don't even really understand the full meaning of Job's offense. For Job to say that God is incorrectly punishing Job (regardless of the softspoken nature of such statements), he says God is not just. And *that* is what God chooses to answer. God's speeches seem harsh to our eyes. But an infinite God can only be offended one way: infinitely. Job *and* his friends are all applying a human standard of justice to almighty God.

Still, how many of us have said to ourselves, "Why me, God?" when something catastrophic happens? To do so is to repeat Job's mistake: not trusting that God is right.

Towards the end of Job 9, Job begins to address his friends again. He shows great insight into human nature here. He sees that humans think that if they just confess something, God will fix them. They believe that a confession is some kind of magic pill with God.[25]

But Job knows better. He defies conventional wisdom. He will not lie just to get back into God's friend list. Any confession would be primarily to shut down his friends' arguments, and it wouldn't be right. He's very defeatist in his attitude about it, but he still won't lie.

In Job 10, Job begins a new tactic: defiantly refusing to give in. He will openly challenge God, thinking, because God has wronged him.

It's an excellent time to remember that Job's emotions are very raw at this point. He's been hurt by what should have been his best friend, God (or so he thinks.) And, his three human friends are not comforting him, but rather hurling baseless accusations.

Indeed, "With friends like that, ...".

---

[25] Actually, a confession is something of a "magic pill" with God: God will forgive all who confess and ask for forgiveness. But, God never promises generally to rid us of the consequences of sin. So, even if the four men had been right that God is punishing Job, confession wouldn't fix Job's predicament.

9: GOD IS SOVEREIGN; OUR JOB IS TO TRUST HIM

(Job 10)

If we study history, we find it littered with the bodies of would-be kings and emperors (such as Hitler and Stalin, mentioned in the previous chapter's opening vignette.) They were people who tried to impose their will on the people around them. In actuality, they were stealing sovereignty from God. Thinking themselves to be great, some have even claimed that they were living gods (Pharoah, Caesar). They were *great, from a human perspective.*

But not from God's perspective. They all share one fate: in the end, they will be dead.

Job's torment is beyond imagining. And it is wearing on his resolve to be God's friend. The one thing above all others that God desires of us is trust. In Job, his faith is wavering. He holds to his integrity, but it's hard doing so.

Job probes the depths of his depression in this speech. "Why then have You brought me out of the womb" (Job 10:18)? "I should have been as though I had not been, carried from womb to tomb" (Job 10:19).

In this speech, Job goes from dismissing Bildad's charges as without merit, then into an unwise boldness against God, and finally back to his severe lamenting.

And what is it that we should learn?

From the speech itself, only the particulars of the moment seem essential. But we must remember the end of the story: God chastises Job severely. He spends roughly a half-hour putting Job in his place. That's more time than is *recorded* of God speaking to *any* other person, including even Jesus. God is very jealous of His sovereignty. He will not allow any other to take it.

God's sovereignty is fundamental to God. Any other person who usurps (or rather, *attempts* to usurp) God's authority will fail. So, arguing with God is pointless; we simply can't win.

Worse, though, if we knew the full truth, we would understand that even when we're mad at God, He still should be in charge.

Yes, God is in charge for a significant reason: it's the only way. Many have put themselves in power over others, like sovereigns of earthly kingdoms. From Nineveh to Nazi Germany, from Sumeria to the Soviet Union, two fates have been shared among them: their leader died, and so did their empires. God's future will not be so. God eternally rules whether we acknowledge it or not.

Further, His judgments are correct, and His plans unerring. He has His reasons. And, much of the time, He does not need to share them with us. So, He doesn't.

Goes doesn't share his reasons with Job. Of all the questions I've asked regarding his life, the biggest is "Why?" I will present some answers, but I guarantee that I don't know all of them. Likewise, Job received no direct answers to this most basic of questions.

Hitler, Stalin, Caesar: they all lost, in the end. And I am very thankful for this: God is still sovereign.

10: INCENDIARY BOMBS
(Job 11)

During World War II, the United States, Great Britain, and Germany all used incendiary bombs to try to get their opponents to give up fighting. It didn't work, but we remember those actions as some of the more unsavory aspects of the war, right alongside nuclear weapon use and death camps.

An incendiary bomb is a bomb designed to start as much stuff on fire as it can upon impact. It's like throwing gasoline on paper and lighting a match.

Welcome to Zophar's first speech. I chose the title of this chapter because Zophar's statements remind me of incendiary bombs. "Shall a multitude of words go unanswered?" "Shall you scoff and none rebuke?" And, "Would that God might speak and open His lips against you" (Job 11:2, 3, 5).

Then he talks about God for a while, only to return to chastising Job halfway through his speech. He spews forth, "For He knows false men" (Job 11:11) and "An idiot will become intelligent when the foal of a donkey is born a man" (Job 11:12). This last is an indirect reference to Job, both the *idiot* and *donkey* parts.

He only speaks for twenty verses, mercifully for us.

Now, after three speeches, each more acidic than the previous, the *friends* have indeed lain out their case. They have no evidence, they've identified no specific sin committed by Job, but they just *know* that Job did something to deserve this. I mean, it only makes sense, right?

Wrong. And, it's probably a good time to remind ourselves of what's happening.

Job suffered unimaginably terrible losses, including health, wealth, family, and peace of mind. He hoped his friends would say something to comfort him, but he meets with only accusations. Zophar is the worst (so far), but Job sees no comfort. Only attacks.

They've made three speeches, each following a statement by Job. Their words have been attacks, attacks just like bombs. Like a scorched-earth policy in war, they leave no room for error in their thinking.

The man has no peace or comfort; they should have presented peace or comfort. Instead, they attacked.

It is also good to remember the end of this story: God dismisses all their arguments with some harsh words. Only God's words are right, and He vindicates Job and rebukes the three friends.

So, despite their saying that Job talks and lies too much, we know that the friends' speeches are the ones short on wisdom and truth. The good guys win, in the end.

> *Incendiary bombs didn't work, but the nations that used them never accepted that. Has Job noticed his friends' wisdom?*

11: JOB'S NOT-SO-GRACIOUS REPLY TO ZOPHAR

(Job 12 – 14)

When I was younger (but not young enough for it to have been an excuse), I used to joke about Romans 12:19 ("Never take your own revenge, beloved, but leave room for the wrath of God, for it is written, 'Vengeance is Mine, I will repay,' says the Lord." I would say, "Oh, I don't want to be mean enough to someone to let God get revenge; I'll just do it myself."

It was silly, and frankly, stupid. But it does remind me that God does say He will execute vengeance for us. It's part of His nature.

Even though He of all people could have claimed a right to it, Jesus did not seek revenge. Instead, He became our model.

Still, how many of us have wished for harm on someone due to how they wronged us? Even Job succumbs to this after Zophar's speech:

Job's response begins with one of my all-time favorite one-liners: "Truly, then you are the people, and with you, wisdom will die" (12:1-2)! This verse is an incisive strike. Job almost certainly sees more holes in Zophar's speech than there are in Swiss cheese. But he also sees the acidic way Zophar spoke to him.

Job claims he is smart, too. He's not inferior to them. And yet, he is a joke to his friends. He was known as the man who called on God, and God answered him. But now, he is just a joke.

In 12:5, Job says, "he who is at ease holds calamity in contempt." This half-verse sentence is worth picking apart a bit. He's making note that people who "have it made" see calamity only at a distance. They insulate themselves from it. He's essentially arguing that his friends can't possibly understand what he's going through because they are keeping themselves at arm's length. They have shown no compassion towards Job; they demonstrated only judgment.

I think he is correct. However, he overlooks the false theology that allows them to be so vitriolic about it, most likely because he accepts that same false theology as accurate.

Now, there's a direct application to modern America here: we are the three friends in this regard. Many in the Church hold to this same false theology, usually without even realizing it. Many in the "prosperity gospel" camp are entrenched in a "we get punished and rewarded on earth for naughty or nice actions" mindset. (For example, if you get sick, then you don't have enough faith.)

But many who do *not* hold to the prosperity position are still holding Job's friends' theology in their hearts. Many a famous preacher has blamed calamities on the sins of the victims (Hurricanes Katrina, Sandy, and Harvey come to mind.) I ask how many non-preacher Christians have done the same thing, at least in their hearts?

Should we judge sin in the Church? Absolutely! "Do you not judge those who are within the church? But those who are outside, God judges. Remove the wicked man from among yourselves" (1 Corinthians 5:12b-13). But we are not to do it as Job's friends are. We have a well-defined process in Matthew 18:15-17. We are also strongly warned to be gentle because we might be guilty of sin as well. "Brethren, even if anyone is caught in any trespass, you who are spiritual, restore such a one in a spirit of gentleness; each one looking to yourself so that you too will not be tempted" (Galatians 6:1).

Now, don't get me wrong: God definitely can and does punish people on earth. But this theology holds that God punishes *on earth* all who do wrong and rewards *on earth* all who do right. As comfortable Americans, it is far too easy for us to slip into this mindset. In the back of our minds, have we thought that those involved in inner-city riots brought it upon themselves? And, further, dare I suggest that some of us have even considered (to ourselves) that they deserve it?

We can become those "who [are] at ease" and "hold calamity in contempt."

Children of God do not fall into this trap. God does not **necessarily** follow that pattern. He only rarely follows that pattern. Furthermore, when He does announce an on-Earth judgment, He always has a purpose. The Bible full of examples of punishment occurring, but they are not even close to the number of sins that occurred. For every disastrous war Israel found itself in, there were countless other nations committing atrocities all over the planet. Did God punish them directly?

No! Eventually, yes, those nations and empires fell. But they also shone with gleaming gold, in some cases for a very long time. Today, some of the most unrighteous people are also some of the most at-ease. And, as Solomon points out, they are not getting punished.

So, the three friends made a grievous error by attributing heinous sin to Job. Still, Job is not significantly at odds with their theology. In his gut, he knows that he has obeyed God at every turn. But Job agrees with his friends that there must be *something* he did wrong to deserve what he has received. He just doesn't know what this something is.

The second central theme that I'm relaying from Job is evident here: do not assume that a calamity that befalls a person results from that person's sin. We cannot say that a catastrophe is a punishment unless God has spoken. The whole book of Job is a blinding light shining on that truth. Please do not fall into this trap.

What Job is thinking here is calling into question this *obvious* truth. God does *not* always punish the wicked. They sometimes do quite well for themselves.

By extension, of course, this theology implies God rewards people for every righteous act. Despite not referring to the theology directly, his three friends believe this: since Job sees punishment rather than rewards from God, Job must have done something wrong. But they have no evidence of anything specific. Job desperately wants to hear their testimony because he believes it himself! But he also knows his own heart and his relationship with God: his conscience is clear.

None of the four men debating here, nor Elihu later, will directly challenge the theology. Job attacks it anecdotally, knowing – or believing – his position before God is good. Very convinced of his upright heart, he is puzzled by God's actions. Mystified and deeply hurt as well, both by God and his friends. He wants answers, but his friends (and God, he thinks) are providing nothing useful.

Job then notes that even the birds and beasts, and even fish declare that God has punished Job. After all, He *is* the One Who gives life to all things, including humanity. It is evident to Job that God is responsible.

Now, remember back that it is Satan who is directly responsible. But God had to grant Satan permission, so in a way, Job is right. In hindsight, we know that God has purposes for everything He does and for everything He does not do. So, God is responsible, despite not having performed the actions Himself.

Then, Job gets back to describing God. He is wise and powerful, and He alone holds counsel and understanding. If He tears down, men will not rebuild it. If He imprisons a man, there is no escape. He causes both droughts and floods[26].

---

[26] Specifically the great Flood of Noah, from the word "inundate" in Job 12:15.

God makes counselors and priests walk barefoot. He makes fools of judges. God frees those in bondage to kings and instead binds the kings themselves. He overthrows those who think they are secure. For poor counselors and advisors, God mutes them. He pours contempt on nobles. He loosens the belt of the mighty (picture a cartoon character cutting the waistband of another person's pants – that's pretty much what he is saying.)

God reveals mysteries in the dark; He brings light to them. He makes nations great and then destroys them. God enlarges nations but later leads them into captivity. Back to the wise, he takes away their wisdom and intellect and makes them stumble around in the darkness. He makes them intoxicated as if they were drunk.

Now *that* is an impressive list of things God does, and that Job acknowledges. But why did he say it at all? It seems to have little to do with Zophar's speech.

But it does. Remember than in the first part of chapter 12, Job was chiding Zophar for thinking he was ignorant. This passage in the second half of the chapter establishes that Job does understand the way things work in the world. Remember that Zophar called him an *idiot* in his speech. Job is making sure nobody believes that.

Job acknowledges that what Zophar (and the other two friends) have said is true. He scolds them for thinking that he might *not* realize it.

But he wants to speak to God Almighty, not these three. He wants to debate with God Himself, not these people who clearly (to Job) are clueless about what's going on. Job has some misplaced pride in these statements. This attitude is going to get him in trouble.

He expands on it as the speeches progress, each time digging the hole a little deeper. If only he could make contact with and debate God, it will force Him to vindicate Job.

Now, if we were present, and did not know about the beginning and the end of the book of Job, perhaps we might be smiling sarcastically and thinking, "Sure thing; God's going to show up and debate you, instead of us. Riiiiiight!" I mean, Job is being pretty bold here, don't you think?

Job is upright because God says so, not because of his understanding of God and of God's ways in the world. His pride is beginning to show through. After the veneer of graciousness has been rubbed away by his friends "comfort." Job is hurting badly. His prosecution of the debate is compromised.

Job claims that the three are smearing him with lies, and they're making pretty lame doctors. He wishes for their silence, which he claims would present more wisdom than their words have. He is right on target with that set of statements.

He begs them to *listen* to his argument. He asks them why they are speaking lies in the name of God. He asks why they are partial in their judgment as they (so they think) debate in God's place.

Job is correct here, as God testifies later. It's not falsehoods that get Job into trouble. What gets him in trouble with God is that he doesn't acknowledge that God can do things God's way, even in Job's life. After all, God ... Is GOD.

It seems unfair, at least to me. Job has been through the wringer. I mean, how many times in history has God said to Satan, "Go ahead, do your worst"?[27] But God's sovereignty is absolute. And He does not take kindly to having his authority undermined. Fortunately for us, God does not deal with us as our folly deserves immediately. How many would survive such an encounter?

God is not obligated to be *fair*. God has bound Himself to be *just*, and that's a whole lot different than fair. Plus, He is just because He has demanded this of Himself. It is His very nature that makes Him just. What Job is going through is no picnic, but God has his reasons.

In 13:9, Job makes a statement that should cause them to shudder (but doesn't): "Will it be well when He examines you?" Recall Jesus' encounter with the woman caught in adultery and the men who accused her in John 8:

> The scribes and the Pharisees brought a woman caught in adultery, and having set her in the center of the court, they said to Him, "Teacher, this woman has been caught in adultery, in the very act. Now in the Law Moses commanded us to stone such women; what then do

---

[27] Twice, actually: regarding Job and regarding Jesus.

you [28] say?" They were saying this, testing Him, so that they might have grounds for accusing Him. But Jesus stooped down and with His finger wrote on the ground. **But when they persisted in asking Him, He straightened up and said to them, "He who is without sin among you, let him be the first to throw a stone at her."** Again He stooped down and wrote on the ground. **When they heard it, they began to go out one by one, beginning with the older ones, and He was left alone,** and the woman, where she was, in the center of the court. (John 8:3-9, emphasis mine)

At the end of that encounter, the men, starting with the oldest, dropped their stones and left. They could not stand in the presence of the Sinless One when confronted with their sin. There was no trial, no big argument, no muss, no fuss. They just left.

The three friends are no different. If they had true wisdom, they would temper their words as they speak further. However, as we shall see, they become even stronger than before as time marches on. It reminds us of Pharoah hardening his heart against God when being commanded by

---

[28] I normally capitalize pronouns that refer to God or Jesus. However, I've left this one lower-case, since the people speaking it (the Pharisees) certainly didn't intend to refer to Jesus as God.

God, through Moses and Aaron, to "Let My People Go!"

Job reminds them that God's majesty will terrify them. All that they have memorably said will become ashes. They'll have no defense when confronted by God.

Job is right on target with this. God *will* judge them harshly. But He will also reestablish Job's relationship with Himself compellingly: by using Job's prayers to absolve the friends' sins. What goes around, comes around, eh?

Job says, "shut up and listen." And see what happens. Then he points out that he is ready to face the music; he will speak his mind and let the consequences fall as they may. Job is getting tired of their speeches; I suspect because they have no value to him.

Then Job prepares himself by leaning on God. Even if God kills Job (for speaking out, which is what Job expects to happen), Job will *still* put his hope in God. And, he knows that his trust in God will ultimately be his salvation. Job knows that the godless man can't make such a statement truthfully. He wants them to listen, and the sentences which follow seem intended to be heard not just by his friends, but also by God.

In a lesser man, such thoughts would be extreme arrogance. But this guy is extraordinary, and he knows it. It's not due to his deeds, primarily, but due to his relationship with God. He has not done anything worthy of this punishment. And, as we know, he has good reason (see chapters 1-2.)

But having chided his friends with their stance before God, Job gives several statements for which Job himself will have to answer when God does speak. He begins by stating that he has formulated his (legal) case. His arguments are ready for the trial. He believes that God will vindicate him.

He applies two conditions to this trial. (Yeah, right, putting constraints on God is going to work. … NOT!) First, he asks that God remove His hand from Job. Second, he asks that God not invoke a fear aura. In other words, he's asking that God fight fairly, according to Job's standards. Then, God can speak (rather magnanimous of Job to permit God to talk), or Job will speak, at God's option.

Although God does not live by our expectations or rules, it turns out that God grants both of these requests. But He does so for His reasons, not due to Job's demands. And further, God requires a much more in-depth answer in response. Job will be woefully unprepared for God's questions.

Job asks God to list Job's sins. He wants to know how he has rebelled against the Almighty. He wants to know why God has hidden Himself from Job and considered Job His enemy. Job is a brittle leaf or the chaff of grain before God. Job wants to know why God even bothers with him, as He has. He is nothing next to the Almighty.

God has written down bitter things about Job in His *ledger*. Job wonders if God is punishing him for something he did in his youth. God has confined and constrained Job until Job is dying alive.

Man doesn't last long. He's like a flower or grass. Or a breath:

> [14]You are just a vapor that appears for a little while and then vanishes away. (James 4:14)

Job is merely noting the truth: we people don't last very long. Especially when compared to God.

God brings judgment on Man, and nobody can be acquitted. Man's days are numbered. He begs God to turn His judgmental gaze away from Job, so he can go about his business and live out the rest of his (short) life.

Do you see the picture here? Job is broken. Broken into pieces, he is, and he cannot see any way out of this predicament. This speech is even more heart-wrenching than his first speech.

When a tree dies, new trees might spring from the roots, even though its stump is dead. Yet when a man dies, he is gone. He never returns. Like evaporating water or a dry river, a man lays down in death and is no more. Even so, he begs for death and also notes that if God grants his request, he won't live again. But he's OK with that. What he has now is worse than death would be, or so he believes.

And, he thinks God will be sorry for what He did to Job. Job implies that God will regret what He did to Job once the realization sets in.

This is a remarkable statement of faith. His relationship with God has made Job confident that

God will miss him once Job is dead. He has the whole theology wrong, but his heart is right. Christians today can have a certain boldness with their relationship with God, but it wasn't exactly healthy in Job's day. I can only think of a handful of people up to this point in history are known to have had this kind of faith: Abel (maybe), Enoch, Noah, Abraham, and Job.

According to Job, God is tracking all Job's sins and has put them in a bag that won't be lost. But even a mountain crumbles away, and rocks move from their place. Water wears down stone, and its torrents wash away the earth. So, the bag full of Job's sins can't last forever, right?

I would just love to give Job a great big man-hug right about now. I pity him.

> *No matter how you slice it, vengeance is something best left to the Sovereign King of Creation. Job even passes this test by not seeking revenge.*

As Job closes out the first round of speeches, do you suppose his friends have seen his pitiful state and softened their stance?

12: ELIPHAZ: "THROWING BULLETS"

(Job 15)

In the early days of movie-making, Hollywood had a love affair with westerns. Some of the biggest names would put out 10+ movies a year in the 1930s.

However, Hollywood didn't have a great deal of knowledge about how real guns firing real bullets work. So, you would see our hero riding at 30 miles an hour with his gun pointed up. Yes, up. Then, he would lower his arm quickly until the barrel was horizontal and then fire. Then he would repeat the process (including raising his arm again.)

It looked cool on-screen, but it was both inaccurate and hazardous as a way of shooting an actual gun.

My dad (who could *shoot) used to call this "throwing bullets" because that's the way it appeared. (Try it for yourself, but, please, use a toy gun.)*

After such a sad and painful speech, one would think that his friends would cut him some slack. But no, Eliphaz is more than a match for any compassion that may have reared its head in his heart. Can't have that, can we now?

He launches into attack immediately, calling Job an old windbag again. Job is full of hot air. He says Job's words are *useless talk* and *not profitable*. These words are a painful, stinging rebuke. But he has no evidence to back it up. It is a statement strictly based upon his preconceived notions: God punishes the wicked while in this world. He doesn't even reply to Job's contention that this isn't true, that some unrighteous people live very well indeed.

He further claims that Job is lying so ferociously that he is hindering reverence and meditation before God. He is probably referring to Job's reverence and reflection. However, he could be referring to those that used to respect Job. In any event, Eliphaz is contending that Job has chosen to use weasel-words vs. simply confessing his evil deeds.

Eliphaz is on a roll now. He claims Job's own words testify against him. As an aside, Job's words *would* testify against him if he were not telling the truth. So, I would be willing to cut Eliphaz a little slack on this point, if only he weren't so acidic in his comments. Remember Job's pitiful state in the last speech; as far as I'm concerned, Eliphaz has no call to respond like this.

Next, he states that Job deludes himself if he thinks he knows all (as Eliphaz himself seems to, from his warped perspective.) He openly wonders if Job isn't claiming some secret knowledge like the 1st and 2nd century Christian heresy Gnosticism[29] would.

He *informs* Job that the three friends include some aged and grey-haired, some older

---

[29] Gnostics believed that they had acquired some secret knowledge that made them superior the 2nd-century Church leadership. It was probably the first Christian cult.

than Job's father. In a culture that values the wisdom of age, this is an important point. And, Eliphaz's words imply that he himself is older than Job by quite a margin. Therefore, he must be right in his pronouncements. That makes sense, doesn't it? As if the elderly/wise can never make mistakes in matters such as this.

Part of his argument is an important point: wisdom *does* come with age, usually. But critically important is this: not all the aged are wise. Only those people for whom the knowledge of God is their foundation become wise. Proverbs 1:7 says, "The fear of the Lord is the beginning of knowledge; fools despise wisdom and instruction." Older people *can* be fools, too. It's just less common.

Also, even those who have learned Godly wisdom are not immune to making wisdom-related errors. Some have gained a little understanding, but have become theologically rigid as if their knowledge were somehow complete. That situation is precisely the one in which Eliphaz and his friends are. Would that we modern Christians do not make the same mistake.

One gets the impression that Eliphaz is simply *throwing bullets*, hoping one hits the target. And, he's having as much success as our intrepid cowboy would have it he shot an actual gun by *throwing bullets*:

Eliphaz asks if the consolations of God aren't enough for Job. He clarifies what comforts he is talking about by saying, "the word spoken gently." There are two significant points here. First, he is claiming to speak for and about God.

And second, they have been *gentle* with Job up until this time.

One should not claim one is speaking for God unless one is speaking for God. And there's a very high probability that if my words are coming from a well-entrenched theology, I may not be speaking for God after all. Getting set in one's ways carries a terrible danger: believing that what one has learned thus far in life includes *all* truth about a matter.

Yes, it is good to study theology and to build a firm foundation. I've been studying Scripture and about Scripture for over four decades. I would say it is even essential, over time. But I should never, *never,* **never** trust that I have uncovered all of God's wisdom on any subject. Jesus' words to the Church at Laodicia serve as a warning to us:

> To the angel of the church in Laodicea write:
>
> "The Amen, the faithful and true Witness, the beginning of the creation of God, says this:
>
> '**I know your deeds, that you are neither cold nor hot**; I wish that you were cold or hot. **So because you are lukewarm and neither hot nor cold, I will spit you out of My mouth. Because you say, 'I am rich, and have become wealthy, and have need of nothing,' and you do not know that you are wretched and

miserable and poor and blind and naked, I advise you to buy from Me gold refined by fire so that you may become rich, and white garments so that you may clothe yourself, and that the shame of your nakedness will not be revealed; and eye salve to anoint your eyes so that you may see. Those whom I love, I reprove and discipline; therefore be zealous and repent. Behold, I stand at the door and knock; if anyone hears My voice and opens the door, I will come in to him and will dine with him, and he with Me. He who overcomes, I will grant to him to sit down with Me on My throne, as I also overcame and sat down with My Father on His throne. **He who has an ear, let him hear what the Spirit says to the churches.**'" (Revelation 3:14-22, emphasis mine)

I think that Eliphaz didn't have an ear to hear.

Eliphaz's second proposition is that they have been gentle. But in your reading, is that your assessment? If that was *gentle*, how does *harsh* appear?

Eliphaz has just announced that he is now taking the gloves off. No more Mr. Nice Guy for him! I guess we're going to find out what *harsh* is:

He then asks how Job can let himself get carried away by such false notions. He has noted that Job's "eyes flashed," probably a reference to his tone of voice and body language. This certainly seems correct, but by Eliphaz turning it into yet another charge against Job, he fails to understand that Job's statements are only wrong if he is lying. Eliphaz *assumes* Job is lying. Based on that premise, his comments are a correct assessment of Job's problems. But since we know that Job is *not* lying, Eliphaz's whole argument is a house of cards.

Can you see what's happening? The two sides have staked out their claims, but the three friends do not listen to Job's statements. And, it seems likely they're not looking to his body language, either.

Then Eliphaz questions how anybody can be pure before God. After all, God doesn't even trust his angels, and the heavens are impure to Him! How much more impure must mortal man be, who drinks sin like water? I have no issue with this statement, but he doesn't stop there. Instead, he claims he has the wisdom of the ages and that his words carry the full weight of their fathers' knowledge.

In writing this book, I sort of am doing that. But I hope I've learned the lesson at the end of the Job's book: never wholly trust my wisdom. I hope and pray that I'm delivering a message from God, not one from Jim.

Someone asked me in a class I was teaching (on Job) how I would have reacted in Eliphaz's shoes. My immediate response was, "not like he did." As I thought about it more, I realized that it is a critical question. Am I *really* learning the lessons? To be willing to put this before the Church as something worthy of time and effort reading it, I better be confident that it's God's will.

I think I've been listening to Him, but I hope I never get as set in my ways as these three men did. Things that violate our concept of what should be are not necessarily wrong. Think about Mary, the mother of Jesus. How possible was it that she was a pregnant virgin? I mean, seriously? Yet, that's what happened.

God is a God of the impossible. I hope I never get so stuck in my ways that I can't see Him moving in a different direction. I can't drag Him with me; I must follow Him.

Eliphaz could have used this lesson.

He continues speaking of the wicked (an apparent reference to Job and evil people like him), that they will always be in pain. Numbered are the days of the ruthless. They are terrified by the sounds around them, and a destroyer will catch up to them.

Still speaking of wicked Job, he notes that Job fears he will never come out of the darkness. He fears that the sword will be his end. He can't find pleasure in food and seems surrounded by overpowering darkness, distress, and anguish.

Folks, this is a blistering attack on Job. He thinks he is doing the right thing by rebuking Job, but enough is enough. These are terrible words to say to a friend, no matter what he has supposedly done. But it gets worse as he explains *why* with a whole series of things that those who thumb their nose at God will see:

- He (futilely) rushes at God carrying what he thinks will protect him, a shield.

- He has grown obese and therefore trusts in his own strength versus God's.
- He lives in desolate houses nobody else would enter.
- He won't get rich, and if he does, his money won't endure.
- His grain will never get ripe.
- He will feel trapped in darkness.
- Flames will destroy his roots and branches.
- Since he trusts emptiness, emptiness will be his reward.
- These things are inevitable.
- If he were a tree, his leaves would not be green.
- Sometimes olive trees and grapevines lose unripe fruit, so Job's fruit will end.
- His fellowship with others is barren.
- Fire consumes his dwellings.
- The wicked create mischief, sin, and deception.

Well, maybe he *was* gentle in the first speech, at least compared to this speech. This one doesn't suffer from being *gentle*. And remember: these are supposedly Job's FRIENDS! I think this is another one of the awful things Satan did to Job: made him lose his friends. At such a gloomy time in his life, it would have been good to have comforting friends. Alas, it is not to be.

Old Hollywood and Job's friends have something in common: they can throw all the bullets they want, but none of them are ever going to hit the mark.

13: JOB'S SAD RESPONSE TO ELIPHAZ

(Job 16 - 17)

In another nod to Hollywood's love for westerns, in the 1950s, they started adding quick-draw competitions. The good guy and the bad guy would face off in the street in a duel to the death.

Squared-off gunfights probably never happened in real life. The average human reaction time is about a quarter second. However, real-life quick-draw artists can draw and fire in less than a tenth of a second. Once one person starts to draw and fire, the other person would have to have already fired to stay alive.

No, the quick-draw duel-in-the-street was created by Hollywood as a way to spice up some westerns.

Now we get to the point where Job starts answering in-kind with the three antagonists. He decides to start drawing and firing just as they have. He begins treating the debate as a quick-draw competition.

He deserves the right to speak to them the same way they have talked to him. On the other hand, he's stooping to their level, which isn't helpful. Still, he's a far better man than I am; it took him 15 chapters to lose his cool. With me, it would have been about 15 seconds.

He calls them windbags (just like they did him.) But even with this insult, he's telling the truth. They are not answering his question, but they *are* trying to solve. They are responding with empty and painful words. Job would prefer if they would just shut up, rather than express pious-sounding words, both wrong and ineffective.

He says he *could* speak like them if he were in their place. But instead, he would strengthen them and lessen their pain. Knowing what we've seen of Job's character, it's understandable that yes, indeed, he would have tried to comfort them and assist them in their pain.

I sense that if Job *did* see a friend living in sin, he would have confronted that person. But he would stick to the facts. His friends are using cruel words instead of facts. It exhausts me just to read it. What would have felt like to be Job at this time? Awful.

It turns out Job just isn't cut out for dueling on their turf. Unable to figure out how to respond to his opponents, he shifts to talking to God. He feels God is angry with Job. He has torn at him and gnashed his teeth at him. Job thinks God handed him over to ruffians and the wicked. I don't believe he's thinking of his friends with this verse, but he could be. It seems more likely he is referring to the Sabeans and other groups that stole his livestock.

With ever-growing images of damage, he is crediting God with harming him. It's like he sees God as a freight train, building up a head of steam more and more strongly, as He attacks Job.

Job has tried to be lowly and contrite, begging God to help him. His face is red from crying. I get the sense that he just can't figure out how to respond anymore because nothing seems to work. He was used to God listening to him; for many years, he lived like that: in concert with God's will. Now, he just doesn't know where to turn.

He claims there is no violence in his hands. We know this is true from God's own words. Pride is not speaking. Job cannot understand why. After living his life having for God, why is God doing this to him?

He requests that the world does not cover up his blood, that his cry sounds for eternity. And, he again claims that God is his witness and advocate. Have you ever heard someone trying to make sure you think something is the truth say, "as God is my witness"? Job is doing the same thing here.

But there's a point of consolation here. Job asks that his cry sound forever. Now, we know that this book is in God's holy Scriptures. We also know that the Scriptures will last forever. Therefore, God *literally* [30] granted this request. Keep this thought in mind as we go forward: Job is in heaven now, and he knows that God honored Job's requests like this one. There *is* light at the end of the tunnel.

Job feels that everyone has left him. And, he's pretty much right, with one significant exception: God Himself is still with Job. We know this, but Job does not. How much more downtrodden can one feel than to think that God

---

[30] Literally may be a word greatly over-used in our culture, but in this case it *literally* applies.

has left him? This feeling is what Jesus felt in the last three hours on the cross. From the negative side, this is what King Saul of Israel felt after disobeying God twice, and God's Spirit left him.

He goes on to request that he could plead with God as he could with a neighbor. What he means is face-to-face. Now, his friends take this as the arrogant ramblings of someone who has severely turned against God, but we know that he's just speaking from his heart.

He feels he will die soon, and then he won't be able to talk to God face-to-face. The trials broke his spirit. All have turned against him. He is in a pit of depression, not to be felt again on Earth until Jesus is on the cross.

But even from the pit of despair into which he has fallen, he still turns to God. He asks God to put down collateral for Job. There are no humans capable or willing, so he asks God for this help.

He also notes that his friends simply don't understand, and further notes that this must be because God is preventing it. They have grievously wronged him; that much is clear. He figuratively claims they've taken a bribe to rebuke Job rather than comfort him. He warns that their children may pay the price for their actions. I doubt an actual inducement happened. But there might as well have been for all the usefulness their words have had.

Job quickly turns back to himself. He notes that he is a byword to the people. The upright are horrified. He is wasting away to nothing, and yet people still won't comfort him.

I get a mental picture of a man holding out his hands, pleading with his friends just to comfort him. And, unfortunately, I also see in my mental image, three men who are piously telling him that both he and his kids deserved what they have received. It's almost like going to a funeral and then criticizing the deceased while at the funeral. It just shouldn't happen like this. But it is.

However, Job won't give up his integrity. He is innocent; he knows this in his heart. He claims he will get more robust and more durable through their having wronged him.

So, he challenges them to try again. Despite having been beaten into submission by God Himself (so he thinks), he doesn't believe they're wise enough to get him to admit to wrongdoing (that he didn't do.) He knows they are uttering useless words, but he also realizes that they haven't finished yet. So, he gives them leave to continue the debate.

However, he is not done with this speech yet. He claims that his friends are making night into day by merely saying it is so. Job is ready for the grave, darkness, and "the worm." The pit will be his father and the worms his mother and sister.

He openly wonders if his hope dies with him and if it will be buried right along with him.

Did you catch that? For his despair to end in death, he fears his hope will be buried with him. This is *desperation* talking. Now, his theology wouldn't allow him to say this, but for him to be despondent because his hope will die with him, it must mean that before all this, Job knew there was more to life than just this life. Amazingly, he still has hope.

This hope is incredibly profound. He officially (theologically) agrees that the wicked get punished and the just rewarded on Earth. Still thinking theologically, death is the end. And yet, his heart *knows* that there is something beyond the grave, or it wouldn't have been so sad for him to think that his hope will die with him.

His relationship with God is so good and so deep that even without knowing (theologically), he *knows* there is more than this life! Folks, he can't say this from Scripture, because the afterlife hasn't referred to yet. Could I have figured out just from Genesis (assuming he had even that)? I think not.

No, this kind of heartfelt hope can only have come from his relationship with God. Here it is, folks: Around 300 years before the Bible even starts to be called a holy book, God has made it clear to one of His best friends that there's more to life than life.

Paul said that one of his foremost goals in life is to know Christ: "**that I may know Him** and the power of His resurrection and the fellowship of His sufferings, being conformed to His death; in order that I may attain to the resurrection from the dead" (Phillipians 3:10-11).

How did Paul learn this truth? The same way Job did: through his relationship with the Almighty. And, we can know it, too, in Christ.

Bildad is about to miss the point of Job's very pointed words completely, but that pales in comparison to what Job's *heart* has just said: he *knows* God! And that knowledge is critical to him. In the depths of his despair, he thinks he's losing it, but the knowledge *is there!*

The message has always been the same: God wants us to belong to Him. That's a tight-knit relationship with a personal God. We attain a relationship with God by faith, but once attained, God will never break it. And, just as with his three friends, nobody *can* destroy it: "My sheep hear My voice, and **I know them**, and they follow Me, and I give eternal life to them, and they will never perish, and **no one will snatch them out of My hand**. My Father, who has given them to Me, is greater than all; and **no one can snatch them out of the Father's hand**." (John 10:27-29, emphasis mine)

Job is at the bottom now. He has almost given up even his hope in the Almighty. But he still has his relationship with God. There is hope, and his gut knows it, even if his eyes can't see it.

> *Shooting quickly is something these guys really should have avoided.*

If only his friends could see this hope in Job's words. If they could, they probably wouldn't make the mistakes they have already made. And Bildad wouldn't say what he is about to say:

14: BILDAD COMES OUT GUNS BLAZING

(Job 18)

Here's my hat-trick nod to Hollywood's love affair with westerns: in some westerns, the hero uses two guns, rather than one. The idea is that our hero is better with two guns than typical bad guys focusing on only one gun.

It looks cool on the screen, but again it's not realistic. Training teaches police and other professionals to use both hands on the weapon and watch their surroundings. If you don't know what is behind your target, don't shoot.

And, never fire multiple shots in quick succession, even with only one gun. Well-trained experts can do it. But even professionals avoid firing multiple rounds unless absolutely necessary.

Bildad starts by coming out with his guns blazing. He begins by saying Job talks too much. He also claims that Job is not showing wisdom and treating his three friends as stupid, as dumb as animals.

Then he claims that Job is destroying himself in anger. While Job may be angry, that's only a manifestation of grief, not a sour heart towards God. Anger is typically a reaction to fear, frustration, or pain[31]. In Job's case, it's clear he is experiencing all three due to his grief and illness, so it's unconscionable for Bildad to claim he is merely shouting at God in anger. Either that or Bildad is a foolish or ignorant person. I don't think he's a fool or ignorant, so that leaves just plain mean.

In fact, in my estimation, Job is showing incredible patience. But his heart is completely broken. He lost all of his children and most of his wealth in the space of just a few minutes. Then, he lost his health sometime later. And, none of these have decreased.

But he hasn't cursed God. His wife asked him to. His friends want him to repent (but, of nothing identifiable.) And his heart just wants to die and get it over.

The *one* thing Job is doing wrong is that he is blaming God, and doing so to twist God's arm to change His will. For this, he will answer. But nothing of what Eliphaz, Bildad, and Zophar have said rings true. They have much more for which they must answer.

Then Bildad colloquially asks, "What? Do you want God to stop the world so you can get off?" The idea is that God should stop running the universe to tend to poor little Job. I can almost sense a sarcastic "boo-hoo" at the end of that. Sarcasm is nasty to someone grieving.

---

[31] There are other reasons for anger, but these are the most common.

Then he spouts a long list of things the wicked have in store for themselves[32].

Bildad has done a decent job with the poetry[33], but what a despicable thing to say to someone who has lost everything. Yes, it's part of his theology, but that's no excuse. Bad theology does not give one license to tear down the hurting.

I've often wondered to myself if the three friends knew what they were saying. How can a friend say such things, and without evidence? Here he is, capping off beautiful poetry with a despicable message. It's hard to believe he was Job's friend.

Yes, Bildad has added another item to his list of sins. But mercifully, at least his speeches are short.

Shooting quickly seems to be Bildad's specialty in this debate. But like an amateur shooter, shooting rapidly will *come back to bite you.*

---

[32] Notice the dualist poetry if you're reading Job along with his book. Each verse says the same thing twice, in different ways. It's kind of like a song that has an echo, except with different elements. In verse 5, his light goes out, and the flame of his fire gives no light. Two lights, each referring to the wicked person's soul, have been snuffed out.

[33] In addition to the dualism, I see chiasms throughout. See Appendix B for a description of chiasms.

15: JOB'S BROKENNESS AS RESPONSE TO BILDAD

(Job 19)

In the movie The Great Escape, *Steve McQueen's character Hilts starts off the film by getting tossed into the* cooler, *a place of solitary confinement in Germany's prison camps.*

McQueen seems oblivious that this is punishment, which grates on the Germans in charge all the more. (Thus, earning him the nickname, "The cooler king.")

Job starts this speech by asking how long they are going to torment him. He claims they have insulted him ten times[34]. But Job, like Hilts in the movie, will not let it deter him that his friends aren't listening.

Job notes, if he has indeed sinned, then that's on his head. He doesn't need them to point

---

[34] As a 21st century American, the "ten times" above would seem to be a count. It is good to remind ourselves that numbers are not necessarily accurate in Job's time, and especially in poetry. Some numbers are meant to be taken exactly as written. For example, Adam really did live to be 930 years old.

But, Job's "ten times" here is poetic and a metaphor. It's simply a phrase that means "a lot". Job didn't bother to count them. In fact, by my count, Bildad has insulted Job seventeen times, just in the poetic stanzas (counting each pair as one insult.) And he also insulted him earlier in this speech, and again several times in his first speech.

it out. It's not their job to be God's mouthpiece to Job. It's between Job and God Himself.

In 19:5-6, Job launches a strong attack against God: "know then that God has wronged me and has closed His net around me." Make no mistake about it: Job is right about Zophar's words being useless, but for his own words against God, Job will also have to answer.

Job has asked for help but received none. God seems to have cut off Job's access to Himself, Job's only real support in all this. God has stripped away Job's honor and ripped him out of the ground like a tree.

And then Job says something he will have to answer for: God has kindled his anger against Job and counts Job as an enemy. God has sent an army to besiege Job.

According to Job, God has also removed Job's support system (friends and relatives.) Nobody wants anything to do with him except these three, and all they want is to *correct* Job. Even the people who live in his house won't go near him. His servants won't answer. He can't kiss his wife, and his brothers despise him. Even little kids hate him. All of his colleagues (probably including these three friends) dislike him. He is wasting away to nothing, escaping only by "the skin of my teeth."[35]

---

[35] Have you heard the phrase "by the skin of your teeth" before? Yes, this is where it comes from; 4000 years old and we still use it today.

He begs his friends to pity him rather than persecuting him. And, he asks if the loss of his skin isn't enough for them.

Note also that he claims God is persecuting him. God is not, but it seems that way to Job. Well, it may look that way, but Job's claim is wrong, and therefore these are words he will have to answer for later.

And then in 19:23-24, he makes a request: "Oh that my words were written! Oh that they were inscribed in a book! That with an iron stylus and lead they were engraved in the rock forever!"

I've said it before: *we* know that God is listening and granted this request because God has placed Job's words into His Bible. Even after time itself is no more, Job's words will remain. Folks, this is a fantastic testimony to how much God loves Job. He's listening, and He is taking action.

I like to think that God prompted Job to write the words of this request. God knew that this story would end up in His Bible, and God isn't faulting Job for what happened to him. God is only going to chastise Job for questioning God's right to do these things; He is not going to chastise Job for having gone through it or any sin that might have led to it.

So, it seems to me that God is giving Job invisible links to God's very presence so that Job will later know that God was with him all through this ordeal. This passage is one such link: prompting Job to pray that his (Job's) words last forever.

The next link is in 19:25-27, where Job makes a statement for the ages: "As for me, I know that my Redeemer lives, and at the last, He will take His stand on the earth. Even after my skin is destroyed, yet from my flesh, I shall see God; whom I myself shall behold, and whom my eyes will see and not another". After all of the pain and grief, fear, and frustration, he says that he will see God face-to-face.

What a man! Even after losing everything, his faith is intact. In his previous speech, he was despairing beyond measure. Yet he still clings to God. Indeed, when He bragged Job up to Satan in chapter one, God *really* knew His man!

There is a lesson for all of us here. How many people have *lost* faith in God when confronted by less hardship? The numbers are legion, including some well-known people.

Folks, never assume that a person's sin is what caused a hardship that befalls a person. Likewise, do not attribute calamity to others as being God's fault. Everything evil in the world exists only because we, as humans collectively, have sinned.

Folks, God didn't want to have to put Job through all this. God *had* to make this story happen, to prevent sinful people (like me) from implying that calamity is automatically a punishment for sin.

God did have another choice, as He always has had. He could simply terminate sinning. At any time, God could decree "no more sin." The problem is that he has to wipe out sinners for that to happen, which means wiping out humanity. It is not *sinning* itself that is the problem; instead, it is the hearts of the people who sin that are the problem. That's you and me.

And God doesn't merely want to snuff us out. From the beginning, God has a plan to redeem us. Yes, we are wretched sinners deserving of death, but God is bigger than that. He offered a one-time sacrifice for all humans if they would only accept it. That sacrifice is Jesus, the only sinless human ever to live. Jesus did not *need* to die. So, when He *willingly* chose to do so, it could change our lives from "dying you will die" (Genesis 2:17, my translation) to alive beyond our wildest imagination's hope.

The blood sacrifices of the Old Testament could not save us. They merely covered over sin, so God didn't have to wipe us out when He confronted us. Jesus' sacrifice, though, essentially replaces all animal sacrifices to God. We no longer need them, so they are no longer relevant to us. What matters now is faith in God.

If you haven't done so in the past, please follow Job's lead and trust Jesus' sacrifice for your soul. There is no more important decision that a human can make.

Anyhow, at this point, Job could have stopped (at verse 27.) He's made his point. But Job knows his friends are wrong and would probably keep attacking him, so he warns them: their words are contrived only to persecute him. Instead, they should be cautious because God does not look kindly on falsehoods, especially when we attribute those words to God.

Knowing the end of the story, this should have a chilling effect. Job is warning them that they are taking their lives into their own hands by falsely accusing him. He warns that God *is* listening, and to more than just Job's words. In the end, Job is proved all-too correct with this warning.

Fortunately for the three friends, God gives them an out from their punishment: if they ask Job to pray for them and ask Job to offer a significant sacrifice on their behalf, God will listen and not do to them according to their folly.

And, Job is their friend. Because, even after all the insults and taunts, Job will indeed offer a sacrifice to God for them, and pray for them, so that they do not have to die at God's hand immediately. They are going to be in a terrifying predicament. And, they will be very grateful that Job, being upright, will not take revenge (as most other people probably would have.)

Job and Hilts have something in common: they both know that, in the end, it will turn out OK.

16: ZOPHAR'S NUCLEAR RESPONSE
(Job 20)

The movie Fail Safe *is about the ramifications of nuclear Armageddon. There's a point beyond which no order can call a plane back that is on an atomic bombing run. This is the "fail safe" point. The idea is that changes to a bombing mission could be a trick of the enemy once they pass a certain point, so the pilots are trained to carry out their mission regardless of words they hear to the contrary, no matter who the speaker claims to be.*

Naturally, some political issue causes the launching of a plane to bomb Moscow. But it was a mistake. So, they do all kinds of things to call it back, including having US planes try to shoot the bomber down. But nothing works, and eventually, Moscow gets bombed.

The Americans' only way out of World War III is to bomb a US city, and they choose New York.

It's a powerful lesson about the seriousness of nuclear arms.

Now, Zophar isn't using real nuclear weapons, but he is seriously ramping up the rhetoric. After his last speech, that's quite an accomplishment. He says that he's been insulted. Job has reproved him (supposedly unjustly), and it bothered him (using words like disquieting, agitation, and reproof.) So, of course, Zophar's "spirit of understanding" forces him to answer.

There is a severe disconnect between Job and the three antagonists. Job has been merely trying to be comforted, but he receives only speculation about his unrighteousness.

I've picked on Job a bit for challenging God's sovereignty, but I've also softened things a bit by noting just how much Job has endured to this point.

The three friends operate from the straightjacket of their theology. This stance causes them to make the fatal (to them) judgment that Job is a wretched sinner worthy of all the pain inflicted on him. But perhaps we should cut them a little slack, too?

I don't think so. The friends' theology was crafted by looking at the world around them and patching God into what they saw. They based their comments on biased versions of God. They were biased away from that which would be garnered by actually getting to know God. So, whether the God they refer to is I AM or not, they've reached a horrible understanding of the One True God.

One of the biggest reasons why the biblical book of Job exists today is because of this bad theology. *All* religions existing since also have gotten it wrong. I include both Christianity and Judaism as part of "all" in that sentence, because many times even sects of those religions, which purport to follow the One True God, still maintain facets of this theology.

I think God needed to give us the book of Job so that people wouldn't make the grievous error of tormenting those on whom calamity has fallen through no fault of their own[36]. As we saw in my summary of Job, God is pretty harsh on them at the end of Job's book. He implies they would be toast if it weren't for God's mercy in accepting – in advance – Job's prayers on their behalf.

Please note that Zophar's whole speech is directly about Job. The style is still poetic, so, even where not clearly directed towards Job, Zophar aims his words towards Job.

Zophar *reminds* Job that all that he is about to say comes from "of old," specifically, it has been in force as long as humanity has been.

Then he launches into a diatribe against the wicked. He says they're only on top of the world for a little while. Even if they seem to have touched the sky, figuratively, it doesn't last.

Of course, the only reason he talks up the wicked's greatness is to dash them to pieces with the rest of his logic. So, he points out that the wicked perish like their garbage. People won't be able to figure out where the wicked went. It's like it was all a dream; he's so far gone. Where he used to live is empty.

Next, he mentions that the sons of the wicked will favor the poor and give back all of the (forgotten) evil man's money. There are two

---

[36]Perhaps I should say, through no DIRECT fault of their own. We all sin, and therefore we all deserve punishment.

problems with this, one stupid and one cruel. The stupid one is that this is rarely true. The sons of the wicked tend to follow in their father's footsteps.

The cruel problem is that Job's sons are all dead. How can they give away his wealth? No, Zophar wants Job to remember that his sons have all been killed, in case he has forgotten. This reference to Job's children is at least the third time one of the friends has cruelly referred to the sons of the wicked, obviously intending to cause Job pain.

It's a good thing it wasn't me to whom they refer. I am not sure I could bring myself to pray for these guys after all they said. But Job is a remarkable man, and I'm sure part of God's plan was to use Job's prayers to nail home the message his friends need to hear: never *assume* that a calamity that befalls a person is a result of that person's sin.

There *is* a judgment day coming, and all the justice these guys imply is currently happening now will be appropriately meted out later by God.

Back to the speech, Zophar says that because the wicked (Job) has oppressed the poor, God will remove all he has, and there won't be anything left for him to steal. All who suffer will fight him in the end. And, there's an unspoken thought: the wicked won't be able to defend themselves, just as Job has failed to protect himself (in Zophar's eyes.)

Finally, Zophar delivers the coup de grace: God will attack the wicked after all the above. God will use iron and bronze weapons. He even includes some disgusting references to what happens to a man pierced by these weapons after someone pulls them back out again. Or when it goes all the way through. Yuck!

Complete darkness: that's what the wicked's treasures become and where they go. The heavens will show all the evil he has done. Even the earth itself will array itself against him. All that the wicked (Job) had collected will flow away (like a river.)

I can see why God uses the phrase "you have not spoken of me what is right, as my servant Job has." (Job 42:7b)

However, there is one saving grace to this speech: it's the last one from Zophar. That's about the only positive thing I can say about it.

It might have been better for both Zophar and the Americans if they hadn't fired off their nukes at all.

17: JOB ASKS ZOPHAR JUST TO LISTEN

(Job 21)

I've met an awful lot of customer service people in my life. Some of them are just there for the paycheck, and you can tell when you speak to them. These don't have an excellent "bedside manner."

Some are starting a career, so they're trying to get it right – by the book. These folks know the rules, but they're reluctant to bend them to keep the customer satisfied.

Some find themselves so focused on the customer that they're always breaking the rules. In other words, they're losing money for the company.

There's a kind of middle ground in there somewhere. The ideal person will bend the rules, but not break them. S/he knows where the line between cost and benefit crosses, and won't cross that line, but they'll get right up to it to help the customer.

Job responds by giving his *customer service people* (his three opponents) a good and right method to console others who are hurting. He knows there is a line they shouldn't cross, but he also knows they're not even getting close to it. Their heart is right (they want to help), but they have no idea how to do it well. Job helps them out after Zophar's speech.

He asks them simply to look at him. He says that look will make them astonished and put their hand over their mouth (in horror.) But he laments, they'll just continue to mock him.

Then, he points out that the wicked still live, and in fact, they get powerful. They see their children and grandchildren, always safely in front of them. Their house is a safe haven, and God does not discipline any of them. The wicked's livestock lives vibrantly.

Their children skip about, playing music and making merry. They spend their days enjoying their wealth. And, when they finally do die, it frequently happens suddenly, with no punishment involved.

To top it off, they despise God. They don't even want to know what God has commanded. They pretend that God is dead or departed, of no interest to them. And, besides, if they *did* pray, they claim it would do no good.

As an aside, Job mentions that the wicked's prosperity is not from themselves, so Job avoids their counsel and wisdom. Instead, it reveals that God shines the sun onto the good and the evil alike. Their fields are watered by the same rain that drops on the grounds of the righteous.

Then Job asks them just how often *does* the lamp of the wicked get snuffed out? How often does calamity befall them? Do they blow away like chaff and straw?

These are rhetorical questions. The three friends have said many things just like these, and Job is challenging them to back it up with some facts. Job has asked this several times, but none of them have supported their statements with facts. Instead, they appeal to the old and wise, to legendary knowledge in force since the beginning of time. But even doing so, they specify no facts or even names of people who have said such things.

Job is rightly pointing out that their whole argument is a house of cards.

Job asks that God would repay the evil person, not their children. After all, he is evil; he may not care what happens to his kids after he dies.

By the way, this statement is a request to God, but he's speaking to the god of the three friends, who doesn't seem to do things the way that Job knows the Lord God Almighty does work. Job knows full well (and has argued so) that the wicked don't get punished at all, usually. Their belief system says the opposite, but Job seems to be learning (as he debates) that things are not as he has always thought. And, we know that God will straighten him out at the end as well.

Then, as if to answer his questions, he notes that nobody can teach God anything, nor can we change his judgments. Interestingly, this statement is actually at odds with his main debating points. He is challenging God's actions, so in effect, he is trying to teach God wisdom. This attitude is another instance of Job needing to learn that God ... Is GOD.

Job says that in truth: One man dies in full strength, at ease in his circumstances. Another dies miserable and discouraged, never tasting anything good. Whether good, evil, or indifferent, their end is all the same. In the end, both lie in the dust, overcome by worms[37].

> **Then to Adam He said, "Because you have listened to the voice of your wife, and have eaten from the tree about which I commanded you, saying, 'You shall not eat from it'; cursed is the ground because of you; in toil you will eat of it all the days of your life. Both thorns and thistles it shall grow for you, and you will eat the plants of the field; by the sweat of your face you will eat bread, till you return to the ground, because from it you were taken; for you are dust, and to dust you shall return."** (Genesis 3:17-19)

The dust Job refers to is the same dust that God refers to: we're all going to someday return to the ground. Death is a fate we all share, the good and the evil alike.

---

[37] This implies that Job knew about the curse, and even hints that he knew the exact wording. It's a good time to remember that Moses compiled and edited Genesis, but he didn't necessarily write it. In fact, Genesis seems to have originally been written by at least 8 and possibly as many as 13 different authors.

God wrote (or dictated) Genesis 1 and maybe part of 2, Adam or Seth wrote Genesis 2 – 4, Noah wrote 6-9, etc. Moses was at least the editor of Genesis. He may have written the whole book from dictation or inspiration from God. Or, he may have compiled from sources we no longer have access to.

Then Job begins a paragraph (Job 21:23-27) by pointing out some things that his friends have stated: Where is the nobleman's house? Have you questioned the nomads? The wicked will ultimately suffer a calamity.

He asks, mockingly, just precisely when this judgment will occur? And, from whom is it coming? No, men will guard his tomb, this wicked one. Even in death, he is safe. Job is correctly noting again that not many evil men come to see their punishment for their deeds.

Since Job rhetorically implies that all of these previous statements are false, he closes the speech by asking how they intend to comfort Job with these words?

> *Job's friends are not doing an excellent job with their customer, Job. They're just doing their job to get by. In the end, it could prove to be fatal for them, except our hero, Job, will do the right thing. He'll do right because he is Job. He gives his all to the task at hand. At the end of the book, that task will be forgiving his friends.*

18: AMAZING GRACE
(Job 22)

When John Newton wrote the song Amazing Grace, it was a simple acknowledgment that he didn't deserve the grace that God had given him. In the movie by the same name, he says he wrote the song only after he lost his eyesight, to which the song refers ("I was blind, but now I see.")

As John Newton learned as he aged (and as many men do), he wasn't as smart as he thought he was. He felt he had done so many wrong things that God could never forgive him. But Newton learned that God's grace is far beyond our ability to sin. He knew how rotten to the core all men are, but He sent His one and only Son to free us from that pit of disgrace. We deserved punishment, but Jesus still paid the price in our place.

Eliphaz tones things down a notch for his final speech. His speech is almost pleading with Job to give up his lying and 'fess up. He's just confident that Job not only has sinned grievously, but that Job knows what the sin is, and is merely being stubborn.

Although he believes he knows God's great grace is enough to heal Job, no matter what he has done, Eliphaz's words are still quite harsh. He finally suggests some salacious sins, which Eliphaz thinks Job *might* have committed and promises that God will forgive and forget if Job will only confess them.

He doesn't know Job well because he implies Job may have withheld generosity to widows and orphans and held back water from the thirsty. We, the readers, know that isn't true because God says so.

So, Eliphaz is offering false hope of God's amazing grace[38], in the hopes of getting Job to stop fighting God. Job responds by telling Eliphaz that his feelings are hurt. All he wants is some compassion, not a diagnosis of sin.

At least in his final speech, Eliphaz tones down the rhetoric a bit. He's mostly talking about God, His love and mercy, wisdom and righteousness, etc. It's all based on a faulty premise (that Job must confess some sin he committed), but at least he isn't launching missiles anymore.

In the end, Eliphaz will be thankful for both God's and Job's ... amazing grace.

---

[38] Actually, the hope is true. But, it's universally true for all believers, not just those who confess specific sins.

19: DEBATE'S END
(Job 23 - 31)

I have never run a marathon, but I know that runners have to train for years to get good at it. And, even with all their training, they are entirely spent at the end.

In Major League Baseball, they play 162 games in a season. The All-Star Break occurs roughly in the middle. Teams have risen from the cellar to the Pennant in just the half-season that comes after the All-Star Break. It's a long season, and everybody knows it. Players, coaches, and fans all know that reversing a poor season can happen because ... it's a long *season.*

Fishers sometimes spend vast amounts of time fishing for that one trophy fish they just know *is out there. Hunters are looking for that monster buck whose head they can mount on their wall.*

Lots of people spend a very long time trying to attain a goal. Some make it to their purpose; many do not. In the first seven speeches by the three antagonists in the debate, they have tried many tactics to get Job to see the *truth* (as they see it) and get right with God.

But they are spent; their *season* is over. Job responds more peacefully to Eliphaz's last speech. In Bildad's third and final speech (which is the closing speech for their side of the debate), it is clear that he has given up.

Instead of telling Job what he needs to do, Bildad simply spends six verses declaring the glory of God and comparing it to the insignificance of Man.

Job then responds with three speeches, none of which are answered by the other three debaters.

In the first speech (chapter 26), Job's response seems to be looking through Bildad's words, and he replies to the intended meaning. But his words are measured. Gone is the acidity of the debate. Gone is the endless bickering and name-calling.

Job knows what Bildad meant, but he says it's no comfort. Job knows who God is and what He wants. And, he knows what his friend wants. But Job declares that he simply cannot confess to what he did not do.

Then, as if to prove that he knows as much about God as Bildad does, he proceeds to document that knowledge.

Job says that God "hangs the earth on nothing." He's not trying to explain the science of gravity; he is merely pointing out that the whole planet on which they reside is just hanging out there in space, exactly where God wants it.

Job notes that God has stuck a lot of water in the sky as clouds, but that the clouds don't burst. God keeps them together.

The pillars of heaven tremble when God speaks. He quiets the sea and shuts down Rahab (Egypt, then the most significant power in the known world.)

He can clear the sky with a breath. Job was merely waxing poetic, but this turns out to be prophetic. In Matthew 8:24-27, Jesus calms a storm that was threatening to overturn the ship. He simply spoke (a breath, if you will) to the wind, and it immediately became calm.

The first verse of chapter 27 says, "Then Job continued his discourse and said, …". This introduction is a break between Job's speech in chapter 26 and the next one in chapters 27-28, just like the end of all previous addresses in this debate. He paused to give Zophar a chance to continue the discussion. Zophar declined, although that detail does not get recorded.

So, Job launched into his second-to-last speech. The tone is different here, as well. This passage was most likely a speech directed at all three of his debate opponents. Something like a "here's your last chance to respond" address.

Job begins with an oath, directed at the whole argument of all of the other three contestants' speeches. Job is making a promise; he refuses to give up his righteousness. What he means by that is that he will not stoop to falsely agreeing with the other three debaters that he has committed some heinous sin. He knows that he has not, and therefore he will not lie. Job says he will maintain his integrity until he dies.

There are two other things of note in this section. Early in this part, Job says God "has taken away my right" and "embittered my soul." Both of these are false, and with the relationship with God that Job made clear in his last two speeches, he should know they are mistaken. Yet, perhaps we should cut him some slack because of all he has suffered. If I compare myself to Job, I know my attitude towards God pales in comparison to Job's.

But God is not a God of relativism. Just because Job's responses are much better than mine would be, does not give him the right to accuse God. God judges each person justly, and against precisely the same standard: His righteousness. Against this standard, we all come up short.

The second thing is that Job says his conscience is clear: "My heart does not reproach any of my days." Here we have a bombshell: he cannot recall a single day where he didn't obey God. My mind recoils against this. If this were the extent of what we know, I would agree with the three friends and say he is lying. Nobody can have a clear conscience, can they?

But we know from the beginning of the book that God Himself says that this is true. Folks, this is one amazing man!

Then he asks God that his enemies be cursed, right along with the wicked and unjust. This statement is pretty bold. And he has included his three friends. Most of all, I think God honors this when he tells the three friends to ask Job to pray for the three. Job will have to forgive them for doing this, but God knows that he will. And Job's forgiveness of them will remove the need for the curse to take hold.

I imagine Job and his friends had quite a visit when these events had run their course. I would love to have been a fly on the wall listening to *that* conversation!

In Job 27:11 ("I will instruct you in the power of God; what is with the Almighty I will not conceal."), Job prophesies that Job would return to his role of admonishing those who need help and that they would listen (again.) The three debaters also made the same prophecy. Somehow though, I don't think they thought in their wildest dreams that the first of the newly-minted learners would be themselves. It just goes to show that God has a sense of humor, even in dramatic situations.

This speech ends with a three-part section, with the "wisdom comes only from God" concept we discussed earlier. Here we have a clear challenge to the three opponents that they simply haven't made their case, and they should do so now or shut up.

In chapter 29:1, there's another pause in Job's speech, as there was in 27:1. He just delivered a final challenge to all three debaters, and then waited to see if they wanted to respond.

They did not, although their reasoning doesn't show up in the text until after Job's last speech: "Then these three men ceased answering Job because he was righteous in his own eyes" (Job 32:1).

At the end of this speech, Job lists off a laundry list of potential sins for which his trials would have been just punishment. And, he notes that he has not done any of them. He goes so far as to be willing to wear the equivalent of an embarrassing sandwich-board around town announcing his guilt if he is found guilty.

But he knows no such moment will come because he hasn't done anything like that.

In the modern world, how many times have we heard a public figure say, "I didn't do anything wrong," only to be proven a liar later? It seems to happen a lot. But it didn't happen with Job.

Humans have filled our world with scandals and scandalous behavior (that aren't always recognized.) Lust and envy and strife and greed: they're all present in abundance. But Job says, "Not me."

He's not a liar, not even white lies. And, God agrees with him.

Folks, this is quite an amazing man. He is a fitting choice for an epic conflict between the master of evil (Satan) and our perfect God. Job still has something to answer for, but overall, he seems to have stood up for himself pretty well. What a guy!

The runner finds himself spent. He thinks he can't take another step. But he does. Again. Because he is Job.

20: ELIHU ENTERS THE FRAY

(Job 32 - 34)

Have you ever been in a meeting with a new guy? I mean that guy who has all the answers and is bursting at the seams to let people know that he does.

Usually, in such situations, the new guy *doesn't know nearly as much as he thinks he does. Frequently, it's embarrassing to have to tell him that he's wrong. Some people take it in stride. Others are hurt by it and don't speak at meetings at all after that.*

At this point, Eliphaz, Bildad, and Zophar stop debating. It is apparent to them that Job is righteous in his own eyes (which would not be a good thing) and set in his ways. They feel that there is no more that they can say that might sway Job to accept *the truth.*

But now, another man will speak. Elihu is this new guy: "But the anger of Elihu the son of Barachel the Buzite, of the family of Ram, burned; against Job his anger burned because he justified himself before God. And his anger burned against his three friends because they had found no answer, and yet had condemned Job" (Job 32:2-3).

But the difference between Elihu and the new guy is that Elihu held his tongue for days or weeks of speeches full of false statements. In that era, people deferred to their elders, and Elihu is no exception.

When he speaks, Elihu does not seem to talk with the same respect as the other four contestants. He probably waited due to his youth; he simply hasn't learned how to be wise in conversation. As we read his thoughts, it becomes clear that he speaks out of anger and without a great deal of preparation.

However, there is one thing we should note before we launch into Elihu's speeches: *God does not condemn him.* While Elihu is present, it is Eliphaz (and his two friends) who is spoken to directly by God. and God has kindled his wrath against them (Job 42:7.)

From this observation, we can draw two possible conclusions. The first would be that Elihu was too young for God to consider guilty. This possibility would be hard to imagine, but it has happened. For example, when the children of Israel were in the desert with Moses, and they failed to go into the promised land due to fear, God judged only those who were "twenty years old or more." (See Exodus 14:20-28.) That would be a stretch of one's imagination, but it's plausible.

Another possibility seems more likely: Elihu was correct. I believe this is why God doesn't mention him.

In any case, this kid is hopping mad, and he wants to make sure the truth shows clearly. If nobody else wants to say it, he will, despite not being older and wiser.

Elihu notes that there is a spirit in men that makes them want to speak (Job 32:8.) And, the Almighty has sometimes given them wisdom as well, despite the age difference. He correctly points out that not all older men are wiser men. Some don't even understand justice, at least not as God does.

Elihu says he waited patiently. He heard their logic and facts. Elihu even paid close attention to them. But he correctly discerns that none of them refuted Job. They gave up, saying effectively, "this is between Job and God; we wash our hands of the matter."

Then in verses 17-20, he asks again for permission to speak. He says that he is full of words, and they threaten to burst out of him like new wine from a new wineskin. He goes on to promise to be impartial and flatter nobody. He even says he doesn't know how to flatter, or his Maker would take him away.

Then, there's no gap between speeches, like there was for the other nineteen discourses. Elihu says, "However now, Job, please hear my speech, and listen to all my words" (33:1). These words indicate that Job may have tried to respond to or interrupt Elihu. But Elihu is burning mad. They will not silence him. But he does promise Job (again) to be impartial.

Then in Job 32:4, he makes a statement shows that one reason why I believe he was correct in his assessments: "The Spirit of God has made me, and the breath of the Almighty gives me life." In other words, he's speaking for God. The other three debaters only hinted that their speeches supposedly came from God. Here, however, Elihu pretty much says his words *are* from God. Folks, don't ever presume to speak for

God unless what you're saying comes from God; it's hazardous.

However, when we get to the judgment chapter, God doesn't mention Elihu. So, I think that God approved of what Elihu had to say[39]. And, at what becomes the end of Elihu's last speech, it almost seems like God interrupts Elihu just before he makes a significant mistake. But I'm getting ahead of myself.

Elihu then quotes Job, "Surely you have spoken in my hearing, and I have heard the sound of your words: 'I am pure, without transgression; I am innocent, and there is no guilt in me.'"

Job did make a bold statement[40], and he will later repent of it. Elihu explains why: it's just not right. *Nobody* is perfect before God on their own. There is always something we can improve, no matter how godly we might be.

Elihu is both right and wrong in this argument. He's right, because nobody stands perfect before God, on their merit. But he's also wrong because God himself declares Job "blameless and upright" (Job 1:8.) God also says that "there is no one like him on earth." Elihu had no way to know that God considered Job blameless, but that doesn't make him right; Elihu is incorrect from an eternal perspective.

---

[39] There are some who think that God inspired Elihu, or even that Elihu is Jesus or an angel. This has to be tempered, however, by some who think Elihu alone is the target of God's anger at the end. So, I prefer to just think Elihu is correct, and not get into those end-case discussions.

[40] Refer to the Appendix for some other statements that I think the debaters would have to answer for.

So, what's the verdict? Is Elihu right or wrong? Well, considering God doesn't mention him when he speaks the judgment on the three, we have to assume that the correct part of Elihu's thoughts was enough to outweigh the incorrect. Does that make God relativistic? No. It just means that when we read the book of Job, we should take Elihu's arguments as basically correct. God is allowing Elihu to speak imperfectly of Himself. And, just like with Job, He has His reasons, I'm sure. But He doesn't have to explain His decisions to us.

At the end of his first speech, Elihu drops a bombshell: "If not, listen to me; keep silent, and I will teach you wisdom." This statement directly answers Job's second-to-last speech, with its emphasis on finding wisdom.

Sometimes ... the new guy gets it right.

21: ELIHU: MY TURN AGAIN
(Job 35)

Solomon is declared by God to be the wisest man who would ever live. God asks Solomon to request from God anything he wanted (1 Kings 4:5.) Solomon prays that he be a wise king to shepherd Israel.

God responds that God would indeed give him wisdom. God says, "Behold, I have given you a wise and discerning heart, **so that there has been no one like you before you, nor shall one like you arise after you**.*" (1 Kings 4:12, emphasis mine) But He goes on to say that even though Solomon didn't ask for riches, long life, and other things for which he might have asked, God would grant them anyhow. The critical thing about Solomon is the great wisdom God gave him.*

Now, Elihu isn't Solomon, but he is displaying some great wisdom here. And, remember, this guy is probably a teenager or young adult.

Elihu pauses to see if anybody wants to challenge his assertions. Waiting is very wise. It also would follow the debate format (allowing both sides to alternate.) But the three friends certainly wouldn't want to interrupt because Elihu has stated (in fewer words) precisely what they've been driving towards the whole time. Or so they think.

They believe that Job is declaring himself pure, as in no sin in his life. But Elihu is speaking more positionally, concerning God's holiness. Elihu must be close enough that they're probably nodding in assent at this point.

I would have thought Job would reply at this point. But he seems to understand that Elihu has a point. Job himself has made this very point earlier. So, it seems, like the humble servant of God that he is, Job is just listening. He wants to see if what Elihu says rings true. And, Elihu is not bashing him left and right as the other three did.

In any event, nobody else speaks up, so Elihu speaks again. He asks the listeners to treat his words like food; if it tastes good, eat it.

But then (possibly without knowing it) he accurately states the reason God is going to show up at the end of the book: "For Job has said, 'I am righteous, but God has taken away my right; should I lie concerning my right?'" (Job 34:5-6a) Then he paraphrases Job again, "For he has said, 'It profits a man nothing when he is pleased with God.'"

He nails what Job has been saying. Job has been questioning God's wisdom. He has also been wondering about all the years he spent being obedient. To this, Elihu has a perfect response: "Far be it from God to do wickedness, and from the Almighty to do wrong."

Elihu states a straightforward truth and is pointing out just how simple it is. He is clearly stating Job's real issue, and at the same time, he criticizes the other three debaters for failing to mention it.

Then, he ends this speech with a blistering conclusion: "'Job speaks without knowledge, and his words are without wisdom. Job ought to be tried to the limit because he answers like wicked men. For he adds rebellion to his sin; he claps his hands among us and multiplies his words against God."

Elihu makes a brief pause, but nobody else speaks. Why would they? The three are almost certainly convicted because they couldn't see this simple truth, and Job is probably seeing what his attitude was, possibly for the first time in these speeches. Elihu is now basically pointing the finger directly at all four of the debaters.

He stresses that Job has asked what profit is there not to sin. But this is something we should never even contemplate. After all, we don't obey God for benefit. We obey Him because He is God.

AND, we follow Him because we're thankful for all He has done. We should give glory to God regardless of whether we approve of His actions or not, knowing that the current situation is in His plan. That doesn't mean we must be thankful for the bad experience we are going through. Instead, we should be grateful for what God has done in the past. This attitude leads our hearts in the right direction.

Back to Elihu, he sharply nails Job by pointing out that the case is before God, and Job must wait for God. But Job has multiplied words rather than just waiting for the Almighty.

Folks, this is precisely Job's issue. There's a lesson for you and me: even when we live through what to us is hard from God, we must still give Him glory. For we know that it will ultimately provide him with praise, and thus is always profitable.

I said earlier that I think Job wrote this book bearing his name. I also believe that he included Elihu's speeches because, painful as they might be, they were right.

Now, in Job 35:14, Elihu hints that God is not coming, or at least He will deal with Job in His timing, not Job's. Stingingly he rebuked Job, and it sets the stage for the culmination of Elihu's speeches.

No, not Solomon. But in this debate, he is indeed in a class by himself.

22: ABOUT GOD ...
(Job 36 - 37)

There's an old song by The Playmates *called* Beep Beep. *It's a story about a Nash Rambler racing a Cadillac. When the song came out in 1958, Cadillacs were the highway's undisputed kings, faster than any other production car. Cadillacs were the muscle cars of the 1950s automobile scene.*

A Nash Rambler, on the other hand, was the original and first successful compact car. Among other things, compacts were not exactly muscle cars, and the Rambler was no exception. It was more like the 98-pound weakling of the auto industry.

The song pokes fun at this by staging a race between a Cadillac and an upstart Rambler. The Rambler pulls up behind the Caddy, clearly challenging the driver, by beeping its horn. Which sounds suspiciously like a child's bicycle horn. (Hence, the name of the song: Beep Beep.) So, the Cadillac driver kicks down the accelerator a little, thinking that would leave the upstart in the dust. It doesn't. The Caddy goes into passing gear, but there's the Rambler right behind him, beeping. They eventually hit 120 (which was mighty fast back then), and the Caddy reaches its limit.

The Rambler pulls up alongside the Caddy, rolls down the window, and asks, "Hey buddy, how can I get this car out of second gear?" And then the listener hears a beep, beep, beep, fading into the distance.

There's a little bit of a contest going on with Elihu. He's the upstart, as the Rambler. He starts what will be his final speech by saying, "Wait for me a little, and I will show you that there is yet more to be said in God's behalf." A pretty bold statement, especially for a youngster. But I, for one, really want to hear what he has to say. He's firing on all cylinders now (and definitely out of second gear!)

He begins with a scary statement, "For truly, my words are not false; one who is perfect in knowledge is with you." *This* statement surely should draw punishment from God. That is *unless* what he has to say is correct. So, I'm going to roll with that assumption.

He goes on to describe God's justice, all-seeing eyes, and His patience to open the ears of those who won't listen.

Then in 36:17-18, he points out that judgment, justice, and wrath *will* come. BUT, there's a ransom. There is an excellent ransom, and he warns Job to "not let the greatness of the ransom turn you aside." Somehow, he understands that God will pardon some people. The promised solution to Man's sin has been in place since the Fall of Man in Genesis 3. Eve named her three (named) sons, all with a view towards the promise from God [41]. Elihu understands this promise, too, and he begs Job not to give up on it just because he can't see it right now.

He warns Job not to join the scoffers. And Job hasn't done so thus far, which Elihu has noticed. Elihu is hoping Job can see the good that will come from God and not the evil that could happen if Job takes his stance much further.

It's almost as if he is trying to say "wait for God," but at the same time, warning that God may not appear.

Then, in Job 36:27 and following, he compares God's wisdom to raindrops coming from clouds. He asks if anybody can "understand the spreading of the [thundering] clouds."

He is using a word picture or parable. Jesus would tell stories that had a moral point, but He would use lessons with which his listeners were familiar. For example, sowing seed or building a tower. Elihu may be doing the same thing.

Let's remember that in two chapters, God is going to answer Job "out of a whirlwind" (Job 38:1.) Elihu is probably noticing that "there's a

---

[41] Sarfati, Jonathan *Genesis Account*, pages 406 and following. Eve named her first son Cain. But, in the Hebrew, she doesn't call him a "son". She calls him "the man, YHWH". This indicates that she believed that Cain was the Messiah promised in the Curse of Genesis 3:15: "And I will put enmity between you and the woman, and between your seed and her seed; He shall bruise you on the head, And you shall bruise him on the heel." She was incorrect in her understanding of when and how this would happen, but she clearly believed it.

storm brewing, a whopper"[42] He says that the lightning and thunder cause his heart to tremble. And, he asks his audience to "Listen closely to the thunder of His voice" (Job 37:2).

The first thirteen verses of chapter 37 are all about a storm, likening it to the voice of God. But he doesn't' actually say that it *is* God, just that God is like a storm. So, I don't think he realizes that the whirlwind to which he is referring, merely as a metaphor, is, in fact, God's vehicle for entering the discussion.

Speaking of a storm, sometimes there is a common effect before a significant storm breaks loose: "the calm before the storm." It's a state where you just know something big is coming because the quiet is just too much. Even the animals are silent. Elihu mentions, "you whose garments are hot" (Job 37:17), so this may be the case in their situation. It's also usually hot in the calm before the storm, especially before the most significant storms. And, if God's going to speak out of a tornado or dust devil, it makes sense that it would be a great storm. I mean, after all, God ... is God!

So, the four debaters, Elihu, and the audience are probably all sitting there, hot and sweaty, and with no breeze to cool them.

He even basically says that God is in a storm in 37:22: "Out of the north comes golden splendor; around God is awesome majesty." Yet,

---

[42] Spoken by the con artist Professor Marvel (Frank Morgan), who would become the Wizard of Oz in Dorothy's dream, in the 1939 classic movie, *Wizard of Oz*.

he follows that up immediately with "The Almighty—we cannot find Him." This statement implies that he doesn't think God is actually in *this* cloud. He's still using it as a metaphor.

Further, by saying, "we cannot find Him," he implies that God doesn't have to show up just because Job has asked.

Then, he seemingly ends his speeches with, "Therefore men fear Him; He does not regard any who are wise of heart." He doesn't think God is coming. And, this is the end of what so far have been spectacular speeches. It's almost as if he was interrupted in the middle of saying that God isn't going to come.

But like the Rambler, God does come. And, Being God, He speaks out of a powerful storm:

23: NOW, I'LL SPEAK – GOD
(Job 38 - 39)

In the movie Twister, *they describe the Fujita Scale used to rate tornado strengths. One of the tornado-chasers says the scale is how much a tornado "eats." It was developed in 1971 by T Theodore Fujita of the University of Chicago. Most nations use this scale, as did the movie*[43].

The scale ranges from 0 to 5. An F0 doesn't do very severe damage. Tree branches get broken, billboards damaged, that kind of thing. An F1 is a bit nastier; they can peel surfaces off of roads.

At the high end, there's the F5. The United States typically only sees 2-3 F5 tornados in a year. They're bad. They're awful. In the movie, when asked how powerful an F5 would be, the answer is "the finger of God." An F5 can obliterate a small city, flattening everything in its mile-wide path.

Now we get to God's set of speeches. So, now might be a good time to recall what these guys might have been feeling. Job has been complaining that God doesn't know what He is doing. The three men have been acidic in their *comforting* of Job and completely missed the point. And, Elihu has just been interrupted after

---

[43] This was true when the movie was released. Today, the United States and many other countries use the "Enhanced Fujita" scale, abbreviated EF0, EF1, etc.

possibly being the most accurate (but also hot-headed.)

He was interrupted by the voice of the One Who simply won't be denied. God speaks from a whirlwind (or tornado or dust devil, in modern terms). We don't know for sure how big and powerful this storm was. After all, this is God, so that it could have been a "finger of God" kind of a whirlwind.

None of the five speakers believed God would come. But God *does* show up to address Job.

So, is God going to answer Job's big question: why did God do all this?

God's first words are, "Who is this that darkens counsel by words without knowledge? Now gird up your loins like a man, and I will ask you, and you instruct Me (Job 38:2-3)! So, I'm thinking the answer to the "Why?" question is, no, God's not going to answer it.

Folks, we're talking about the Almighty. He doesn't spend His time explaining His actions. He is all-powerful, all-knowing, and all-good. He doesn't *need* to reveal Himself. It's our job to figure it out! More on that subject later.

For now, God asks a series of questions that the listeners had no chance of answering. Most of them are not answerable today, even though some are scientific questions.

The first is a good example: "Where were you when I laid the foundation of the earth?" Well, technically, we *can* answer it: nowhere. So, it's more of a rhetorical question than an unanswerable one.

But the next one, we moderns should be able to answer, right? "On what were its bases sunk?"

Wait, I don't even know what *bases* are! They were probably pillars or foundation stones of some kind. And, just as likely, they were destroyed or moved out of their role as a foundation in the Flood. So, no, we can't answer that.

In 38:8-11, He asks Who put the shore on the oceans. The first time I read this, I thought, well, duh, the coast has to exist; it's the boundary between land and sea. But as I thought more about it, it's a much deeper question. God isn't asking for the obvious answer (Himself.) He's asking *why* and *when*. I can answer *when*: at the end of the Flood of Noah[44]. Why? That's beyond me. And, the question is beyond Job, which is God's point.

He asks where light lives. And he follows up by asking where darkness lives. Where is snow stored? (We can answer that one today, but Job couldn't.) Does the rain have a father or mother?

Can we move constellations in the night sky? Can we direct lightning? (Sort of; lightning rods will help. But don't bet your life on one.)

Can we do the hunting for lions? (Yeah, right. We would *become* the prey if we tried!)

---

[44] God also placed the shores where they were when he created dry land on day 3 of Creation, in Genesis 1:9: "Then God said, 'Let the waters below the heavens be gathered into one place, and let the dry land appear.'; and it was so." But, the ocean/land boundary by the time of Job had been radically altered by the Flood.

God gives a humorous description of ostriches but ends with the fact that she can easily outrun a horse, laughing as she does so. And, speaking of horses, God mentions that He's the one Who gave them their mighty strength.

One after another, the questions are intended for one purpose: to put Job in his place.

This questioning bothered me for a long time. It doesn't seem fair. But as I studied the book more and more, I realized that God is very close to Job. They have a *tight* relationship. Job has always obeyed God, more than any other man on earth (at the time.)

So, this line of questioning from God isn't to harm Job or hurt his feelings. It's so that Job can understand that "God's ways are not our ways" (Isaiah 55:9, paraphrased).

Further, we must surrender to this truth: God ... is God. He is the Almighty Sovereign of the universe. His works are always good because that is His nature. So, even when bad things happen to us, He has His reasons, and we should not argue with them.

Like damage done by an F5 tornado, the sovereignty of God can be hard to accept. For us, and Job:

24: JOB REPLIES: WHATEVER
(Job 40:6 – 41)

In my home, many times, I, as a parent, had to invoke my authority over the kids. When they were young, they eventually accepted it and did what they were supposed to (most of the time.)

But when they got older, they would sometimes tell me, "Whatever." "Whatever" meant they weren't going to argue anymore, but they were still thinking themselves right. Many families have banned "whatever" in those kinds of discussions. Our family didn't go quite that far, but it certainly was annoying to end a conversation that way.

Now God pauses and asks Job to respond. Actually, "demands" is more like it: "Then the LORD said to Job, 'Will the faultfinder contend with the Almighty? Let him who reproves God answer it'" (40:1-2).

Job has to be feeling down about this time. But his response is not to surrender. It's more like, "Whatever." He isn't responding so much as he is shutting up. It's almost like he knew something like this would happen.

His reply isn't repentance. But God didn't ask him to repent. God asked him to present his case, and Job declined. So, God will need a better response. He *does* want Job to surrender completely. After all, He *is* God.

BET YOU CAN'T TOP THESE BAD BOYS

To do so, God brings out his final argument. First, he clearly states that He requires a surrender. But God states it in reverse. He says that if Job can match His power, then God will confess to Job. Laughable as this may seem, He goes on to present two creatures that display His tremendous power, Behemoth and Leviathan.

We don't know what these two creatures were. But we do have the descriptions God gives them. The first is the Behemoth. The name itself is plural, but He's not talking about many behema; He uses a majestic plural. Picture a king on a throne about to give a judgment on a criminal. If he's in a good mood, he might say, "Though your crime is serious, *we* are in a benevolent mood. Thus, *we* pardon you by *our* good graces." The king is referring to himself in the plural, to show his majesty. Behemoth is similarly named.

So, what was Behemoth? In a study Bible, it might say "hippo or elephant." Let's see how those fit. Behemoth (40:15-24):

A. Was made at the same time as Man.
B. Eats grass.
C. Has powerful legs and belly.
D. Has a tail that sways like a Cedar tree.
E. Has bones like tubes of bronze.
F. Has limbs like bars of iron.
G. Is "first" of the ways of God. "First" here means the biggest and toughest (but not meanest or chronologically first) creature ever.

H. Lies under lotus plants, in marshes and rivers.
I. If the river it's in floods, Behemoth ignores it.
J. Nobody can capture or tame Behemoth.
K. A behemoth lives in or near the Jordan River.

Bullet A says it's a land animal because it was created when Adam was (day 6 of creation.) That narrows it down a bit, but not much. The same is true with B & C; they don't narrow things down much.

But then we come to D (40:17), which says he bends his tail like a cedar. The phrase "bends his tail" is typical of moving a tail like a dog might wag his tail. The term "like a cedar" refers to cedar trees in that area of the world, known for their exceptional height. They sway in the wind. Many Bibles have a note in the margins that this could be an elephant or hippo. An elephant has a tail like a small rope, and a hippo's tail is a flap of skin. So, we can rule those out.

Thus, no living creature comes close to matching Behemoth. So, what animals *do* match that description? The list includes extinct crocodiles, alligators, and long-tailed dinosaurs[45]. Some sea creatures might fit, too, but we already know that Behemoth lived on land.

---

[45] Just because dinosaurs are thought by most to have been extinct for millions of years, That is incorrect. They most likely would still be alive in Job's day. It's only a few hundred years after Noah released them from the Ark.

E & F aren't much help. Any large creature could have metaphorically strong bones and limbs.

The phrase "He is the first of the ways of God." is telling. The Hebrew word means *best* or *chief*. In other words, this is the undisputed pinnacle of land creatures. After all, it's God Who says this about Behemoth. So, we can assume that this is one of the largest and most challenging animals ever to live. Neither an elephant nor a hippo comes even close to that. They are some of the most massive land creatures alive TODAY, but God has stated He is referring to *all* animals.

Bullet H, lying under lotus plants or living in marshes, doesn't narrow things down, but they would eliminate elephants if they were still in the running.

A flooding river would dislodge most creatures, but several dinosaur species were large enough that they could have withstood a significant flood. This stability would be more valuable for a flood of the Jordan because it isn't that large of a river (compared to, say, the Amazon, Nile, or Mississippi.)

Since we've already ruled out all creatures alive today, the fact that nobody can tame or capture one isn't helpful. But I could easily imagine a sauropod dinosaur being hard to catch. It's not something I would particularly enjoy attempting.

So, my best guess is a sauropod dinosaur[46].

---

[46] We can deduce from God's usage and Job's reaction that this is a creature with which Job was familiar.

In chapter 41, God describes Leviathan. The description takes the whole chapter. Leviathan was a creature that lived or prowled in water. The most common suggestion is a crocodile. However, this creature is one nobody can hunt, for it is just too fierce. Ancient Egyptians pursued crocodiles, and since Job was well-traveled, he would certainly know this.

Leviathan was virtually invulnerable and ferocious in the extreme. Whatever Leviathan was, it's not something a man could effectively hunt (41:8.) Even the sight of it can overpower a man (41:9.)

But perhaps its most unique feature is that it bellows smoke, steam, and fire from its mouth and nose. There are very few creatures alive today that the description "fire-breathing" fits. The bombardier beetle comes to mind, but they fire their explosives out the rear, not through nostrils. Some lizards *sneeze* out salt, but none of those are large enough to qualify as impressive.

Also, no weapon made by humans (at that time) could pierce it. In an anthropomorphism[47], God says it laughs at any such attempts[48].

The best candidate I could find is a *sarcosuchus imperator*, a monstrous crocodile-

---

It's not likely Job would surrender after hearing of a creature for the first time. It's not going to be impressive to him if he doesn't know what it is.

[47] An anthropomorphism is a figure of speech where the speaker assigns human qualities to a non-human creature or object.

[48] God could have meant that it really does laugh, but that's not required by the text.

like creature that inhabited both land and sea. It's extinct now, but it was twice as long as the longest modern crocodiles. What is interesting about this guy is that there are cavities inside its skull. These could have been repositories of volatile chemicals, similar to a bombardier beetle. Of course, the bombardier beetle fires its explosive mix from the rear, but it's an excellent example that spewing out *fire* isn't so far-fetched as it might seem.

As with Behemoth, Leviathan is extinct. But the same argument used for Behemoth applies to Leviathan: it wasn't extinct in Job's time. Otherwise, it wouldn't cause Job to surrender; it would still be just another "Whatever" situation.

Let's hope Job doesn't respond with whatever again.

25: ABOUT GOD'S MERCY
(Job 42)

In the movie Independence Day, *aides propose nuclear weapons as a possible weapon against the alien attacks. But, the aliens have stationed themselves over U.S. cities. Bill Pullman plays his role as President well, agonizing over the decision.*

But there comes the point where the President gets into telepathic contact with the aliens. This contact causes him to realize that there is no negotiating with the aliens. All they want is to destroy life on Earth and strip it of all its resources. So, he makes the fateful decision to nuke the alien ships, even though they are over our cities.

They nuke one of the ships, but it causes no damage. It's a moment when the audience thinks all is lost.

Similarly to the President, Job must be thinking that it's all over now. God has put him in his place. To a reader, this is possibly the most depressing point in the story. There seems to be no hope.

God laid it all on the line, saying essentially, "Job, if you can top these, then I (God) will admit you're right."

Of course, Job can't tame these creatures[49]. Leviathan was virtually immune to attack from puny humans, and Behemoth ignored us[50]. Thus, Job surrenders completely.

When I first read Job's confession of complete surrender to God, it made me sad. That's because I didn't understand what it meant. Back then, "surrender" was a bad word to me; I don't like to lose. And I thought God was a God of love. Surrender (to me) implied a despot or dictator, almost the opposite of a loving person.

But now I know that surrender to God means I'm surrendering to *God*, which means I'm also submitting to His character qualities, power, righteousness, etc. God is good; therefore,

---

[49] An important point here is that Job KNEW about these creatures. Picture God using the equivalent Orcs and Nazgul from Tolkien's *Lord of the Rings* trilogy, instead of real creatures. Fictional creatures simply could not cause Job to surrender. He would not have been impressed at all. But, he went from a resigned "whatever" response, to absolute and complete surrender, once God describes these guys.

Therefore, we can deduce that these creatures were known to Job. This then makes more sense out of 40:23, "If a river rages, he is not alarmed; he is confident, though the Jordan rushes to his mouth." The Jordan is more than an example. It is a river Job would be familiar with, since he is well-travelled. Further, it means there was one of these creatures living there, another fact that Job must have known. So, even though they supposedly died out millions of years ago, they were actually alive during Job's time.

[50] Who knows what would have happened if Leviathan and Behemoth met in open combat? But, since one is land-based and the other sea-based, that will have to remain an open question.

surrendering to Him is good. God is righteous (always right); therefore, submitting to Him is the right thing to do. God is all-powerful; surrendering to Him means I fall under His protection as well as His authority.

It had to have been hard for Job. I imagine he was brokenhearted at God's response. For, when Job makes his confession in 42:1-6, he doesn't realize that God has accepted him back into His good graces. We won't see this until God turns His attention to the follies of Job's three friends. Fortunately for Job, that happens immediately:

God speaks to Eliphaz the Temanite[51] and says, "My wrath is kindled against you and against your two friends..." (Job 42:7). Wow! Put yourself into their sandals for a bit. They gave eight long speeches, delivered over days or weeks. They believed the words they spoke were valid. But God is angry. God is in a wrathful mood. God's wrath (not just anger) is burning against them[52]. And, folks, God's wrath is a terrifying thing to behold. In Numbers 16, 14,700 people died when God's wrath went forth. In Numbers 25, 24,000 people died, and the number would have been higher had it not been for Phinehas's quick actions (nephew of Moses and son of Aaron), who interceded for the people. In 2 Chronicles 29-36, Judah is nearly wiped out and is sent into captivity

---

[51] This is a strong indicator that Eliphaz was the leader of the three, and probably the eldest as well.

[52] This is another indicator that Elihu had things right, for God is essentially mirroring Elihu's attitude, only more strongly.

in Babylon due to God's wrath. I could show many more examples, but you get the idea: God's wrath is a truly terrifying thing.

Back to Job's friends, this had to be terrifying for them. Remember, we're not talking about a prophet, which would be scary enough. God *himself* is there, speaking from a tornado. And, He's not just upset. His *wrath* is on fire.

Their folly deserves death, and even worse. But in a stunning twist, God offers them a path of mercy: they should ask Job to provide a sacrifice for them and pray for them. If they do, and if Job makes the offering and prayer, then God will forgive them.

The three friends, who berated Job for days or weeks now have only one hope of survival[53]: ask Job to stand between them and the Holy God. My, how the tables have turned. In seconds they went from actively humbling Job to a position of absolute terror in the presence of the Sovereign God of the universe.

At this point, Job must forgive them himself if he's going to offer a sacrifice and prayer on their behalf. Fortunately for them, he does both.

But two other things happened at the same time. First, Job now realizes that he is again God's *servant*, a term of great endearment when God uses it. It doesn't get any better than that. And, second, Job's character would have its chance to shine. Job had to forgive his friends immediately. There's no way he could offer a sacrifice for them

---

[53] Even their eternal destiny was at risk.

unless he first forgave them. Turnabout is indeed fair play, but forgiveness ... who would have guessed?

Finally, God restores Job's fortunes. He receives double of everything he owned before Satan destroyed it. And God granted him another ten children [54], among which are his three daughters named [55] Jemimah, Keziah, and Keren-happuch. They were said to be the fairest in the land. Talk about a storybook ending!

> *Job is at the point of total despair and feels that all is lost, just like the President. But we find that the Almighty God of the universe had a plan after all. In the end, the good guy wins.*

---

[54] A question arises as to why Job's wealth was doubled, but his number of children was not. I'll cover this later.

[55] Telling the names of daughters was unusual in those days.

26: AN ANCIENT PLAN

The story is over, but I promised an answer to Job's repeatedly stated question, "Why?" and several others.

I've repeatedly stated two big reasons shown many times in the text of Job, which both partially answer the "Why?" question:

- God ... Is GOD. We must completely surrender to Him. Surrender may not be a pleasant thought until we realize entirely just to Whom it is we capitulate.
- Don't Blame the Victim. Unless God Himself states that the purpose of a disaster is punishment, we should *never assume* that it is punishment. For, we can kindle the wrath of God when we do so, especially when we say we are speaking in His Name.

The above two lessons apply to us today. But there's another reason not directly stated in the text: to teach us. We need to remember that this incident takes place long before there is a full understanding of God's dealings. (In fact, there never is a time when we will *fully* understand God's ways.)

So, one purpose is that this whole episode ends up in Scripture to teach us. God's Word lives forever. Therefore, Job's story will live forever. So, nobody who follows should ever make the same mistakes Job and his friends made[56].

Humans make a habit of ascribing things to God about which He has nothing to do. This habit frequently happens on both sides of a calamity. Neither the victim nor onlookers should think that a catastrophe is a punishment. It *could* be, but unless God says so, we must not *assume* that it is.

The book of Job is another part of God's progressive revelation about Himself to His creation, Humans. That plan had gone on since before time began, and it will continue after time itself is gone. In the Garden in Eden, Adam and Eve knew that they deserved to die. And yet, God puts mercy into the very act of dying: forcing us to live forever in this rotten, sinful state would be hell on earth.

God's plan included the death and rebirth of Jesus in the Curse itself: "I will put enmity between ... your seed and her seed. He shall bruise your head, and you shall bruise him on the heel" (Genesis 3:15). The promised Messiah would be the seed of the woman; the devil could only wound him. But the serpent would be utterly crushed by the Messiah.

While Eve understood that the promise existed, she did not know when this would happen. She named her first son Cain in a way that declares Eve thought he could be the promised

---

[56] We will make those mistakes, because it's our nature to sin. Nevertheless, we shouldn't make them.

Savior[57]. (She probably figured out fairly quickly that Cain wasn't exactly savior material. Hence her name for Abel, which means vanity. It wasn't going to be *her* son that saved humanity.[58])

She didn't understand the principle that the Messiah would be from a woman, not the regular union of a man and a woman. This fact wouldn't be understood until at least Isaiah's time[59]: "Therefore the Lord Himself will give you a sign: behold, a virgin will be with child and bear a son, and she will call His name Immanuel" (Isaiah 7:14).

The book of Job intends to move humanity from ignorance about God. God expects us to learn about Him and have a relationship with God. It is an essential book because we humans would otherwise make Job and his three friends' mistakes, and without the book, we would never know how wrong we are.

From the beginning of time to the end of time, in fact, beyond both ends of time itself, God has at least one principal purpose in His heart: to love. He has wanted to love humans, the pinnacle of creation. Jesus died so that we could love Him back. For, in our sinful state, we are incapable of loving God, unless He first loves us. Jesus destroyed that corrupt state's eternal and inevitable conclusion by dying Himself in our place.

---

[57] Sarfati, Dr. Jonathan, *The Genesis Account*, pgs 406-409.
[58] Ibid, pg 409
[59] Isaiah wrote in the 700s BC.

And, just as He did with Job, Eliphaz, Bildad, and Zophar, God wants to be our friend. He offers a path to mercy, just as He does in the epilog to Job's book. My prayer for all readers of this book is that it causes us to draw closer to the Almighty God of the Universe ... as His friend.

Now, two final questions need answering. First, why was Job's wealth doubled, but his family size was not?

But it was. Wealth is temporal; we can't take it with us. But humans are immortal. Where is Job now? He's in Heaven with his Creator and Friend.

But wouldn't his children also be there, with him? It's hard to imagine how they wouldn't be. So, in Heaven, Job has 20 children; thus, his family doubled in size. (However, my wife commented that she feels sorry for Job's wife!)

Finally, there's a question I haven't asked before, but you might have: Why wouldn't God just tell Job in advance about what He intended?

The first and most straightforward answer is that Satan would object that that's not a fair test.

But a far more critical answer comes from the previous question's answer: Job is in Heaven now. Heaven is timeless, so Job is with God and *has been* with God the whole time. And, in the presence of the Almighty, he almost certainly agrees with the actions God took. Thus, I think Job *did* agree with God. He just didn't realize it until many years later.

27: REUNITED

The story is over now. But there may still be more to be said.

This chapter is entirely fiction, the way things might have happened in Heaven after Job passes on from this life.

I tried to use what I know from the book of Job, and what I know about God Himself from the whole Bible, to weave a story of how the early conversations Job has in Heaven might have gone.

All good things come to an end, and so it is with Job's life. Little did he know that immediately after he died, he would come to a much more glorious place: heaven, the place where God Himself lives.

When Job makes the transition, his ten children and the servants who died in the calamities greet him. They all start talking at once. "Master!" "Daddy!" "Father!" And they all come up and give Job a round of hugs for the ages. "You wouldn't believe it here, Dad. But I think our Lord Himself wants to tell you about it."

As the King of Kings arrives, they all fall to their knees in worship.

Then the Lord turns to Job and says, "You are right to worship, but you may stand in My presence. For you have set a standard with your life unmatched by the vast majority of Mankind." The Lord then bids the rest to take seats (which suddenly appear around Job.)

Job rises, a bit puzzled. But his heart has been perplexed for the last 140 years. A question has vexed him ever since the ordeal: "Why?" He had guessed at many answers, but now he might get to know the full answer. Still, questioning God isn't something to be done lightly (if he learned *anything* from his ordeals, he indeed learned that!)

The Lord, ever looking into Job's eyes, says, "You may ask your question now."

Without hesitation, Job asks: "Why?"

"My dear servant and friend, you ask the wrong question. Ask instead, 'Why *me*?'"

Job is puzzled even more by this, but as he ponders the situation, God gently interrupts: "I needed someone that I *knew* would survive the ordeal *with his faith intact*. Of all the men who ever lived, I chose you because I knew you would not succumb to the pressure and turn away from Me."

Job doesn't notice it, but as the Lord speaks to him, more people trickle in to join his first ten children around Job and God.

Job is even more puzzled, but as he ponders these statements, he begins to piece things together in his mind.

"Yes." the Lord said. "I needed a man to hold up because I needed to attack a problem my people would have throughout time: they think calamities are punishments. Your three friends and even you held to this understanding.

"However, calamities are not always direct punishments. The vast majority of tragedies are only indirect punishments. They are consequences of sin, but not just the sins of the people affected by the calamity. No, disasters come because all humanity turned away from Me. Once Adam sinned against Me, the entire universe began to die with him. Humans had caused Me to remove My sustaining power from the Universe, subjecting it and everything in it to decay and death.

"People had to die eventually. People would also get sick and suffer losses. But others would see these things and think it was punishment. I saw their pride welling up in them: 'I must be right before God because He didn't punish *me* like that.'

"They believed that it was their goodness that protected themselves from calamity. Thus, they elevated themselves over their traumatized neighbors.

"Don't get Me wrong; there were times when I directly punished those who deserved it. But I always told my prophets in advance what I was going to do. I always hope to save."

Job is so fixated upon God's words and presence that he does not see the arena-like seating that has arisen around the two of them. Thousands, no millions of people are filling the seats that appear just as they arrive to listen.

"Look around you, Job." Job notices the rings of seats, now filled by Job's wife, all twenty children, Eliphaz, Bildad, Zophar, and Elihu. And, around that, he sees crowds of people, listening to God's every word.

"See there?" God says, pointing at the crowd. "From there," God states, as he pivots and sweeps across almost the entire arena, "all the way around to over here, are millions of people who needed to hear what your story should have told them.

"But over here," He says, pointing to a much smaller group of people, "are the ones who read your book, and understood that they should not be prideful; calamities happen to all people, not just those who deserve it."

At this, the millions who failed to learn the lesson, including Job's three friends, turn towards those who understood and heeded the message, breaking out into loud ovation. Eliphaz slapped Elihu on the back, saying, "*Well done*, my friend!" Even God Himself smiled at the applause.

"I see now," Job said. "You needed to make sure people, at least those who had ears to hear, would listen and drop their pride. You paid me a *great* honor by choosing me out of all the people on Earth, to be Your object lesson. I also understand now that You couldn't tell me in advance, lest that liar, Satan, claim you cheated (again.)

"It was a great plan, Lord. While you don't need me to say it, I will: I permit you to put me through those calamities. (As if You needed permission!)"

Again, Job started to drop to his knees to worship, but God catches him and says, "Keep standing." And there followed another thunderous applause, by everybody in heaven, even the angels. And, God gave Job a great big bear-hug.

APPENDIX

WORDS FROM NINETEEN DEBATE SPEECHES

I'm going to highlight many of the verses that the men speak that might incur judgment. We know that God will render three decisions in the end. No, *"render judgments"* is too harsh. He states of the facts, but with overwhelming force (duh! He's God!)

I'll deal with these in the same order God deals with them:

- God deals with Job's statements challenging God's authority to do things His way.
- He deals with the false words of the other three debaters.
- He officially states that Job has spoken truthfully, and restores Job.

In this section, I will present the passages where the debaters have said words, which I believe God has heard and deals with when He speaks.

Please note that there is a great deal of interpretation involved in this; feel free to disagree. This section is intended more as food for thought than any kind of precise theology. And, God Himself does not tell us which are the words to which He reacts. But it might help us just think about things for a while by speculating a bit as to which statements God is referring.

JOB'S CONTENTIOUS WORDS

First, we'll look over some of Job's words that challenged God's right to be God:

In Job 6:4, Job contends that God has shot him full of poison arrows. It's Satan that has performed the deed, but God allowed him to do it. Some might consider these words, since they're false, to be accusing God. But I'm not going to hold this against him. There's no way he could know the full details (yet), and God *did* allow it.

Many examples of this kind of thinking exist; I'm ignoring the rest of this chapter.

In 7:11, Job says he will complain in the bitterness of his soul. Complaining about circumstances is always a problem since it is God who allows all situations.

In 7:17-18, Job claims that God has put him under a magnifying glass, and tries Job every moment. While this is true, it's not God's primary purpose; God isn't judging Job, but Job thinks He is.

In 9:15, Job states that if he were right, he still couldn't answer God. It is a mistake to believe that we can be correct when contending against God.

In 9:20-21, Job notes that God would still declare him guilty even if he were guiltless. (And, then he says he *is* innocent!) But Job can't be guiltless in his own estimation. Although he knows he hasn't done exceedingly wicked things, he still needs to offer sacrifices.

Now, we know God Himself has declared Job "blameless and innocent." But Job shouldn't make that claim for himself. He should trust God enough that, in the end, God will come to his defense.

In 9:32-35, he says that there's no umpire between God and Job. But the Messiah, Jesus, stands between Job and God the Righteous Judge. But Job can't know that; it won't come into force until 2000 years later. So, I am willing to cut Job a little slack here.

However, in the last verse of the chapter, Job says that he will speak if God stops punishing him. But when God speaks, Job goes silent. *Nobody* can stand before God unless God purifies them first. So, there's no way Job would be able to do this, and he should have known it and not said that.

In 10:3, Job claims that God looks favorably on the schemes of the wicked. Job is doing this only to be poetic[60]. Nevertheless, these are words one should not say about God. He never looks on evil positively, because His very nature excludes all evil.

---

[60] His words are a poetic style called dualism. This is where two stanzas speak of the same concept, but with different words. For example, "My car's red paint is brilliant; it gleams like the sun." In Job's poetry, it's contrasting dualism, so a better example could be ""My car's red paint is brilliant; my neighbor's car is barely noticable.

In 12:2, Job responds by insulting his debate opponents. Now, Zophar's speech was almost nuclear in its fieriness, so I can certainly understand the change in Job's demeanor. Still, it's not very nice of him. So, this might be something about which God is upset. (Job also responds insultingly in his speeches after this one.)

In 16:9-16, he claims God is angry with him and is thus punishing him.

In 16:17, he claims there is no violence in his hands, and that his prayer is pure. This statement implies that God has made a mistake. But in 19, he lands the gem: "My advocate is on high." So, I temper my understanding of this being something God about which will be calling him to account. A lot of the statements Job makes imply a mistake on God's part. It's almost like he is treating God as two different people, one who judges, sometimes mistakenly, and one who advocates for Job. Gee, I guess that makes him the second[61] recorded Trinitarian Christian.

In 19:6, he outright states the "God has wronged me." This verse is definitely on the list of things God for which calls him to account. It is simply not possible that God can wrong anybody. It violates His very nature. His character (which includes His acts) *defines* right. Job continues this

---

[61] Eve literally says that her son, Cain, is the Lord in Genesis 4:1. She was wrong, but it shows that she believed that God would send a Messiah, and that that Messiah would be the Lord Himself. This makes Eve the first recorded Trinitarian Christian.

line of thinking all the way to verse 22, so it's not out of context.

In 21:7-26, Job questions why the wicked still live. In addition to saying that God made a mistake punishing Job, God also erred by not punishing the wicked. The rest of the chapter seems to be on the same topic (God's error), but from verse 27 on, he speaks to the three debaters.

In 23:4-7, Job states that he would present his case to God if God were there. But then God allows just that (in Job 40). Yet Job is so awed by the presence of the Almighty that he doesn't present any case.

I believe this passage (and others like it) are the reason God pauses between His litany of unanswerable questions[62] and His presentation of two majestic creatures [63] as His final argument[64]. He wanted Job to remember the words that Job has spoken.

In 23:8-9 and following, Job says that God is not around him. But both he and we know that God is always around. So, this is a false statement about God. He made it for poetic reasons, but it's still wrong.

In the first half of 24:1, Job seems to be saying God has not remembered Job's life of godliness. But the rest of the chapter clarifies this is a statement of indictment against God's failure

---

[62] Chapters 38 and 39.
[63] Behemoth in chapter 40 and Leviathan in chapter 41.
[64] God's presentation of these two examples of His greatness and power are what ultimately cause Job to totally surrender to God.

to recognize the sins of the wicked. In either case, though, Job is saying God isn't judging things correctly.

In 27:2, Job claims God has taken away his right and embittered his soul. But we have no rights before God, so that's wrong. And, if Job's soul has become poisoned, it's Job who did the poisoning.

But this is immediately followed by a statement that he refuses to accept the doctrine of the three debaters and admit to wrongdoing that he has supposedly done.

In 29:2, in Job's final speech, he says that God used to watch over him (and implies that God is not doing so now.) God indeed watched over him; it is Satan's opening salvo in his argument against Job's virtue. But what's *not* true is that God has stopped caring. To say so contradicts his own words elsewhere.

In most of chapter 30, Job is insulting his debate opponents. But most of it is both hyperbole and correct: his friends *have* been making those false claims about Job; they just weren't as specific. So while I'm sure God disapproves of the tone, I refer this is not one of the things about which God speaks.

All of chapter 31 is a series of statements about bad sins Job claims he has not committed. Now, God could count this against him, since "all have sinned and fall short of the glory of God" (Romans 3:23.) However, I don't think Job did any of these specifically. They aren't a claim to sinlessness, as could be perceived. Instead, they are simply a list of heinous sins, which Job declares he has not committed. So, I don't believe God is referring to these at all. (In fact, I think that if any *were* present in Job's life, God *would* have stated them. But He doesn't, strongly implying that they do not exist in Job's life. In effect, the whole episode seems to be more like fine-tuning Job's relationship with God.)

THE FRIENDS' CONTENTIOUS WORDS

Next, we'll look over the false statements by the three debaters opposing Job.

Chapter 4:7 states the question, "Who ever perished being innocent?" and "Where were the upright destroyed?" This argument is the foundation of all three debaters' contentions, so we'll take a closer look than we otherwise might.

First, let's note that nobody is truly innocent. As true believers in God, He has granted us justification. But that's because Jesus paid the price for our pardon, about which Eliphaz doesn't know. So, Eliphaz isn't starting from a valid start point.

Second, nobody has perished or seen destruction [65]. So, his argument is empty. But remember that they're making their arguments poetically, and it was more critical for them to write good poetry than to have ironclad ideas.

And third, Job has been declared "blameless and upright" by God Himself. It doesn't get any better than that, but of course, our friends

---

[65] Job's children died, but as we saw in the main part of the book, they weren't destroyed.

don't know that. Still, they *do* know Job, and they know he is a man of high integrity. They should just trust him on that basis.

In 4:12-21, Eliphaz tells us how he got his facts: a stealthy, whispered voice, and disturbing thoughts in visions of the night. He was terrified. As a spirit passed his face, his hair stood on end. The voice declared that nobody is just before God (true) Nobody can be pure before God (also true).

Then the voice says, "He puts no trust even in His servants." This statement is false. God knows who will be trustworthy and who will not be.

I could go further with this spirit's contention, but now we know whose side the spirit is on: Satan's. For only satanic powers will speak falsehoods about God.

Furthermore, we have another hint: this one mixed truth with a lie. That's the hallmark of Satan himself. So, while we can't prove it, it seems likely that Satan is doing more than just hurting Job. He's also acting to turn his friends against him.

Shudder!

In 5:1 (and many other places), Eliphaz claims that nobody will help Job. But since this is the first time, we must recall that he believes Job has sinned dramatically, and that Job knows that he has sinned. So, it's a small thing for nobody to pay attention to him.

In 5:2-7, he tells what happens to such people, and it's not pretty. He mentions death, curses, dead family (ouch!), no deliverer, oppression, no food or wealth, etc.

But in 5:8 to the end of the chapter, he goes on about how Job should seek God. By this, he means Job should repent. Recall from Job's speeches how he refuses to admit wrongdoing. Job is addressing this very thought by Eliphaz.

In chapter 8, Bildad says that Job is wrong. God does not pervert justice (vs. 3.) He tells Job to ask of the aged and wise, and they'll let him know: turn back to God (i.e., repent again.)

Bildad uses all kinds of metaphors to describe Job's plight. For example, in verse 14, he says that Job's "trust [is] a spider's web." In other words, Job's thoughts are garbage.

In chapter 11, Zophar speaks angrily. He calls Job a liar and a scoffer. He also says that God *forgets* a part of Job's iniquity. This statement is blatantly false; God removes our sin far from us, but He doesn't forget it. An all-knowing God cannot forget. He must erase, and only *after* judgment.

Zophar's whole speech is harsh. And, a good portion of it isn't correct, either. All three are wrong-headed, but Zophar takes the cake. (But somehow it gets worse in his second speech!)

Eliphaz starts his second speech (15:1-6) with insults, even worse than his first speech. But in 15:4, he states that Job hinders other people in their meditations before God. And, in verse 5, he claims that it is guilt that has trained Job's tongue.

Also, because this is the second speech, I want to make sure folks notice that he provides zero evidence. *All* of his words are entire guesses. So, in 42:8, when God says, "… you have not spoken of Me what is right ..." this is certainly something to which God is referring.

In 15:16, there's a whopper: God "puts no trust in His holy ones (probably angels), and even the heavens are not pure in His sight." Recall back in chapter 4 that the first half is almost exactly what the dark spirit told him. The second half seems to be expounding upon this vicious lie.

In 15:20 is a centerpiece of the last half of this speech, namely that punishment always comes on wicked men (just like Job, right?). Job has already stated that all one needs to do is look around. Looking will clarify that the wicked do *not* always get punished (within their earthly lifetimes.) Eliphaz doesn't bother to answer that charge; he simply states as fact (again) God always punishes the wicked. It is tough to imagine how he can say this. Anybody who checks (as he advocates) will undoubtedly find evil people doing just wonderfully.

No, God *will* punish. But in people's entire lives, not just the earthly component of that life. However, remember that in this era, people didn't have an understanding of the afterlife. So, to Eliphaz, this is a logical deduction of his concept of life: when it's over, it's over. So, for God to be just, He *must* punish them here on Earth.

There's a principle here that needs to be understood: a theology that leads to sin is not a good reason to sin. It is never correct to sin, no matter how piously one believes he acts. Attacking Job is sinful, and having a strong belief does not exonerate the debaters.

In 18:2a, we see a hint of Job's true piety in the words of Bildad: "How long will you hunt for words?" In other words, "Job, you're taking too long on your speeches."

Since when is it wrong to be careful with one's words? These words hint that Bildad isn't taking as long as Job did to write his speech. So, now Job's crime is that he's too careful with his words?

Bildad should have immediately apologized for that. But instead, he drones on about how God's going to punish the wicked. There's also the implication (as with all three debaters' speeches) that God is punishing Job right now.

In chapter 20, Zophar gets his second and (thankfully) last speech. It's just one insult after another. Oh, and mixed in with statements of how God judges the wicked like Job. Every single verse contains either an insult or an account of what God is doing to evil people. Real peaches like "the venom of cobras [is] within him" (20:14b), "For he has oppressed and forsaken the poor" (20:19a), and "God will send His fierce anger on him" (20:23.)

I'm sure glad we don't have to read any more of his words.

In 22:1-11, we have the last of the attacking speeches. Here Eliphaz says basically what he and the others have already said: Job has significantly sinned, he *knows* he has sinned, but won't admit it. Therefore, God is punishing Job, as all the other wicked people will be.

In 22:12-20, more warnings about what happens to bad guys.

And, at 22:21-30, he appeals to Job to repent. This passage is the only *nice* speech portion in all of the three debaters' first seven speeches. It seems that they are losing steam by this point.

JOB'S WORDS THAT ARE JUST GEMS

And now, we get to my favorite part of the debate: gems from the lips of Job[66]. In other words, things Job says that tell something positive about himself or God.

In 6:3b, Job explains that his words have been rash (agreeing with Eliphaz's speech). But Job explains that it's because of the depth of suffering he has endured.

In 6:9, Job concludes a lamentation by wishing that God would just kill him. But in 6:10, he states one thing consoles him: he has not denied the words of God.

What he is referring to is the tendency by people in great distress to lash out at God. I know I have done that many times.

But Job has not done that, even though he has rightly[67] stated that God is behind things.

---

[66] I tried to find any gems (as I call them) delivered by the three other debaters. Alas, I could not find anything other than Bildad's sign-off speech (which is just a "whatever" ending, not a real gem.)

[67] Satan is actually doing the hurtful, but God allowed it.

Instead, he holds it as a consolation that he has remained pure, despite his rash words (6:3.)

9:5-12 declares the greatness of God. For instance, in 9:9, Job notes that God made the Bear, Orion, the Pleiades, and the sky's constellations. In other words, everything seen in the night sky comes from the hand of the Almighty.

Many people, faced with far less than what Job was facing, thought about taking their own lives. But in 10:1, Job says he hates his life, yet he doesn't even consider killing himself. Instead, he says he will "give full vent to [his] complaint."

In a way, he's asking God to take his life, but he won't do that himself. We get the impression that he's asking God to blast him with lightning or something. I wonder what went through his mind as the storm, from which God would speak in chapter 38, approached while Elihu was delivering his speech.

In 10:7, he declares to God that God Himself knows that Job is not guilty. I wish that I could say that with a clear conscience. No wonder Satan took notice; this guy is impressive.

Job 12:2 has one of the greatest insults ever delivered: "Truly then, you are the people, and with you, wisdom will die!" It's not displaying good character, but it is funny reading it right after Zophar gives his first slash-and-burn speech.

Still responding to Zophar, 12:13-25 extols the greatness of God again. Included among these, he says, "he makes fools of judges." His three friends have put themselves into the judges' chair regarding Job, so I think he's indirectly referring to them.

In 13:6-7, Job asks his opponents to just listen to Job's words, so they don't speak for God *unjustly*. Job pleads with them to watch out because they are telling falsehoods in God's name. They will later interpret it as another boast from Job, but he pleads for their very souls. Speaking falsely for God is a significant offense to God, and they are heaping judgment upon themselves by doing it. And, we find at the end of the book that Job is right: God is angry over what they said about Him.

At 13:15, Job says, "Though He slay me, I will hope in Him." Wow. Just, wow. No matter what happens, he will trust God. This attitude is just fantastic, mainly because he knew next to nothing about the afterlife (as we know it.) Yet here, in the middle of greatest despair, he trusts his Father in Heaven.

In 17:9, he repeats a similar sentiment: "Nevertheless, the righteous will hold to his way, and he who has clean hands will grow stronger and stronger." This comment comes sandwiched in the middle of a speech lamenting his brokenness, but he refuses to give up. He knows that, in the end, God will be his friend.

In 19:23-24, Job asks that his words get written in a book, engraved in lead on stone, forever. And God honored that request. Job's comments are part of God's written Word, the Bible, and the Bible will last forever. God literally fulfilled that request, and our study of Job's book is testimony to that.

It goes further: Job asked why many times, but never got an answer. But we *do* have the answer, or one of them: to keep people from blaming victims.

One of the great purposes of the book of Job is to prevent people from making the three debaters' errors. In a nutshell, they blamed the victim for something that happened to him. God can and does judge people on this planet, but it is not our place to make such a judgment. Therefore Job's book is a warning to the rest of us: calamity does not equal punishment (unless God Himself has so declared it).

Now, that is quite a truth. But Job follows it up with something even better: "As for me, I know that my Redeemer lives, and at the last, He will take His stand on the earth. Even after my skin is destroyed, yet from my flesh, I shall see God" (Job 19:25-26). That's quite a statement from a guy who doesn't know anything about the afterlife. So, from where does this come?

It could only come from his lifelong friendship with and personal knowledge of the Holy One. Even Job doesn't understand this fact; most people thought of God as creator, life-giver, judge, jury, and executioner (among other things.) But they didn't consider friendship with God. Yet, even without *knowing* it, Job's words clearly show that he was God's friend.

Folks, it doesn't get any better than this. We may have problems spending time with God and His Word. I know I struggle with maintaining a quality devotional life. But here, Job is so close to God that he utters one for the ages, and it's just matter-of-fact to him.

> As an aside, showing the depth of Job's knowledge, in 26:10, Job accurately describes the terminator between night and day on earth. Recall from your science classes in school that the sun shines on half the globe, while the other half remains dark. Scientists call the line where sunlight and darkness meet the *terminator*. Job correctly describes this as a circle, which means he knew the Earth is a sphere.
>
> A little earlier, at 26:7, Job said, "He hangs the earth on nothing." Modern people would be hard-pressed to state the earth's place in the solar system better than this, with only six words.
>
> Put together these two verses, and it becomes clear that Job knew the earth was a sphere hanging in space. I doubt his understanding of outer space was very good, but this is a pretty remarkable declaration of knowledge from a supposedly primitive person. One thing is clear: the ancients were *not* primitive.

Chapter 27 is the second of Job's final three speeches. In 27:7, Job shows that he knows there *will* come a judgment day and that his opponents will not fare well then. Job is correct in this prophecy, but the timing comes much sooner than any of them could have predicted: in chapter 42. But our merciful God gives them a way to be redeemed: ask Job to pray for them; God will listen to "[His] servant Job."

Chapter 28:1-11 tells of mining the earth, the riches we can extract from it, and things like that. He shows a clear understanding of mining practices[68]. But the purpose of telling about the wealth mining can take from the earth is different: he compares it to *wisdom*.

Wisdom cannot be so easily mined, he claims in 28:12-22. In fact, at 28:22, he says that even the grave only hears a report about wisdom. So, from where *does* wisdom come?

It comes from God. Like Solomon declared as his purpose for writing the book of Proverbs, Job shows that he knows wisdom comes only from God. In Job 28:28, he utters the wonder sentence, "Behold, the fear of the Lord, that is wisdom." If that seems familiar, Solomon will write something similar a thousand years later, "The fear of the Lord is the beginning of knowledge" (Proverbs 1:7a). It's even possible that Solomon was paraphrasing Job.

In chapter 31 (the final chapter of Job's closing speech), Job makes a series of "If I've done this, then ..." statements, where "this" is some sin. Job is making a vow that he has not done any of these things and that God should punish Him severely if he's lying. He didn't, and God didn't.

---

[68] This is another tidbit that shows he wasn't primitive or ignorant

BIBLIOGRAPHY

Barnes, Albert (1942, May) *Barnes' Notes On The Old and New Testaments*; Job I

Barnes, Albert (1942, May) *Barnes' Notes On The Old and New Testaments*; Job II

Sarfati, Jonathan D. (2015, April) *The Genesis Account*

BibleGateway.com

BlueLetterBible.org

The Lockman Foundation, *New American Standard Bible*, 1995 Updated Edition

Made in the USA
Monee, IL
08 December 2020